Kids Are Consumers, Too!

Real-World Reading and Language Arts

Jan Fair

and
Mary Melvin
Carol Bantz
Kate Vause

▲▼ Addison-Wesley Publishing Company
Menlo Park, California • Reading, Massachusetts • New York
Don Mills, Ontario • Wokingham, England • Amsterdam • Bonn
Sydney • Singapore • Tokyo • Madrid • Bogotá • Santiago • San Juan

Acknowledgments

Special thanks to C. Stuart Brewster, Phyllis Chiado, Bernard Cohen, David Corley, Barbara Eggert, Lois Fowkes, Carole Gould, Cora Menatti, Bruce Payne, Judy Radshaw, and Priscilla Cox Samii for their help and support on this project.

Thanks also to Jane Lathrop Stanford Middle School, June Schiller, Summer School Principal (Palo Alto, CA), and Selby Lane School, Joanne Hendricks, Principal (Redwood City, CA), where the photos in this book were taken.

Special thanks to the following teachers and students:

Teachers: Maurice Benetua, Joyce McClements, Susan Morss

Students: Tony Burciago, Stephanie Chancellor, Shane Coronado, Jennifer Covert, Ben Crosson, Kimberley Dervis, Eric Fair-Layman, Stephanie Fair-Layman, Jeffrey Hart, Cassie Hayden, Rance Hayes, Taylor House, Eric Kalkbrenner, Heather Kehres, Tobye Lau, Alice Moberg, Klara Ng, Jason Porzse, Michael Power, Alexandra Ramirez, Metra Sadri, Rachel Sheridan, Assad Waathiq

This book is published by the Addison-Wesley Innovative Division.

Illustrations: Steve Osborn

Photographs on pages 3 and 205 by Tim Davis.

All other photographs provided expressly for the publisher by Wayland Lee, Addison-Wesley Publishing Company, Inc.

ISBN-0-201-22227-2

BCDEFGH- A L-8932109

About the Authors

Jan Fair has taught real-world reading and language arts activities as a classroom teacher in six states—in rural, suburban, and urban schools. She has authored numerous books, poems, magazine articles, and educational materials and is a speaker and consultant for school districts as well as community and parent groups throughout the United States and Canada. Ms. Fair is currently teaching at Allan Hancock College in Santa Maria, California, and is the director of AEM, Association for Education and Motivation, which conducts motivational and educational seminars nationwide.

Mary Melvin has more than twenty years of experience teaching reading and language arts to elementary students. Her interest in using the real world as the focus for learning has been evident in her elementary and college classes as well as in staff development workshops and presentations at regional and national conferences. Dr. Melvin currently teaches graduate and undergraduate courses in reading and language arts at Miami University in Hamilton, Ohio, and is an active member of the International Reading Association and the National Council of Teachers of English.

Carol Bantz is a teacher at Fairlawn Elementary School in Santa Maria, California, where her approach to teaching has involved real-world experiences at a variety of grade levels. She is a Mentor Teacher for the school district and serves on the Language Arts Action Team as a consultant/workshop leader for effective teaching strategies. Ms. Bantz also teaches Children's Literature at Allan Hancock College.

Kate Vause has extensive experience as a classroom teacher, both at the primary and intermediate levels. She is currently teaching at Alvin Avenue Elementary School in Santa Maria, California. Her interest in real-world learning experiences is an extension of her work in initiating and carrying through new educational projects in the classroom as a teacher and advisor. Ms. Vause is active in curriculum development for the Santa Maria Elementary School District and currently serves as the leader of the district's Spelling and Handwriting Action Team.

CONTENTS

Reading and Language Arts Skills Covered in the Book   ix
Chart of Curricular Areas Related to Activities   xi
Introduction   xiii
    What You'll Find in This Book   xiv
        The Book's Organization   xiv
        Organization of the Activity Chapters   xiv
        Format of the Activities   xv
        Underlying Themes   xvi

PART 1. SKILL AREA ACTIVITIES   1

Chapter 1. Reading   3

  1. Reading Apple Wheat Crackles   5
  2. An *A* to *Z* Activity   13
  3. Index Treasure Hunt   15
  4. Message on a Bottle   16
  5. Abbreviated Ad Art   19
  6. Monitoring Your Magazine   20
  7. This Move Is Classified   22
  8. A Twisted Memory Teaser   25
  9. The Warranty Game   29
10. Sell Your Setting   33
11. Quick and Easy   37
    A. Keep Your Eyes on the *Y*'s   37
    B. A-B-Seeds   37
    C. Vowels—Eat 'Em Up!   37
    D. Blend Spending   38
    E. Classy Syllables   38
    F. Where the Action Is   38
    G. Just the Facts, Please   38

Chapter 2. Writing   39

  1. Ad-Libs   41
  2. It Pays to Advertise   45
  3. Create-a-Catalog   49
  4. To Whom It May Concern   51
  5. For a Code, Take Lemon Syrup   53
  6. Dial M-Y P-H-O-N-E Number   57
  7. A Classy Phone Book   61
  8. Name That Word   63
  9. Walk Softly and Carry a Sharp Pencil   66
10. Quick and Easy   68
    A. Shopping List   68
    B. Food for Thought   68
    C. A Chalkboard Collage of Feelings   69

D. Story Stretch 69
E. Compose Yourself 69
F. Brand Name Words 70
G. Supermarket Anagrams 70
H. Lost and Found 70
I. The Mail Must Go Through 71

Chapter 3. Listening and Speaking 73

1. Take a Message, Please 75
2. A Picture Is Worth a Thousand Words! 79
3. Go with the Flow Chart 80
4. Buyer Beware! 83
5. Tune In to Feelings 84
6. Meaningful Music 85
7. Taste and Tell 86
8. The Energy User Game 89
9. Quick and Easy 91
A. I Scream for Ice Cream 91
B. A Word from Our Sponsor 91
C. Consumer Charades 91
D. Phone Fun-damentals 92
E. Speak Out! 92
F. What You "Auto" Know About Insurance 92
G. Commercials and Jazzy Jingles 93
H. Name That Slogan! 93
I. Introducing You! 94

PART 2. APPLICATION ACTIVITIES 95

Chapter 4. Restaurants, Stores, and Supermarkets 97

1. Good Eating Reading 99
2. Pick a Present for a Pal 103
3. The "I Care" Game 109
4. Let Your Fingers Do the Jogging 111
5. Name, Rank, and Cereal Number 115
6. Mind Designs 121
7. Old and Neglected Ads 122
8. Supermarket B-I-M-G-O 123
9. Quick and Easy 127
A. Words for Sale 127
B. To Buy or Not to Buy 127
C. Supermarket Riddles 127
D. Catalog Sketch 128
E. Ad Appeal 128
F. International Foods 128
G. A Brand New Car 128
H. A Generic Activity 129
I. Within Reach 129

Chapter 5. Careers, Jobs, and Chores 131

1. Career Pursuit 133
2. Patent Pending 134

3. Now You're in Business! 137
4. Career Connection—The Interview 139
5. Apply Yourself—Get a Job! 141
6. Step to Success—Write a Résumé 145
7. Classroom Chores—A Problem? 149
8. Plan Ahead 151
9. Quick and Easy 153
   A. Making Mad Money 153
   B. Who Works Here? 153
   C. I'm Thinking of a Career 153
   D. Creative Licenses 153
   E. 101 Uses 154
   F. You're the Boss! 154
   G. Job Search 154
   H. Baby Sitter's Idea Kit 154
   I. Job Skills 155

Chapter 6. Entertainment and Leisure Time 157

1. Comic Strip Punctuation 159
2. Sports Page Synonyms 163
3. The Guide Game 165
4. Good Sport Sporting Goods 167
5. Hobbies and Interests 171
6. Let It Snow! 172
7. Way to Go! 173
8. Quick and Easy 177
   A. Popular TV Shows 177
   B. My Very Own Computer 177
   C. Toying with Toys 177
   D. Spelling Words Go Up, Up, and Away 177
   E. Compounding the Fun 178
   F. For Your Viewing Pleasure 178
   G. 25 Words or Less 178

Chapter 7. Holidays and Special Occasions 179

1. Greeting Cards—Say It with Style 181
2. Holiday Hang-Ups! 187
3. Poet-Tree and Other Decorations 188
4. Cut-Ups! 193
5. So It's Your Birthday! 194
6. A Holiday Feast 199
7. Quick and Easy 200
   A. New Year's Resolutions 200
   B. Valentine Couplets 200
   C. St. Patrick's Green All Over 200
   D. "Eggstra" Advice for Spring 200
   E. For Mom and Dad 201
   F. Be Patriotic—Vote 201
   G. Healthy Halloween! 201
   H. Thanks! 201
   I. Make a List and Check It Twice! 201
   J. Crazy Mixed-Up Greetings 202

PART 3. PROJECTS   **203**

Chapter 8. Projects   **205**

1. Holiday Telegrams: A First-Class Business   207
2. Let's Advertise Nationwide   213
3. Meet the Press: Getting to Know the Newspaper   219
4. Let's Form a Job Club   223
5. Career Day   226
6. Progress Report: A Straight-*A* School   229

PART 4. SUGGESTIONS FOR USING THIS BOOK   **235**

Chapter 9. Tips for Teachers   **237**

Using the Activities   238
     Choosing an Activity   238
     Planning the Activity   240
     Adapting Activities   241
     Using Activities in Related Curricular Areas   242
Special Features   242
     Quick and Easy Activities   242
     Real-World Reading and Language Arts Games   243
     Real-World Materials   244
     Problem-Solving Approach   244
     Use of Computers   244
     Activities to Do at Home   244
Special Uses   245
     Staff Development   245
     Substitute Teachers   245

PART 5. MATERIALS AND RESOURCES   **247**

Chapter 10. Materials and Resources   **249**

General Suggestions for Materials and Resources   250
     Ways to Get Materials   250
     Ways to Use Materials   252
     Guest Speakers   253
     Field Trips   253
     An Alternative to Guest Speakers and Field Trips   254
Real-World Materials Chart   254
Specific Suggestions for Materials and Resources   256
Real-World Games Chart   274
Teaching Aids   275
Award Certificates   278
Song   280
Skills Index   283

READING AND LANGUAGE ARTS SKILLS COVERED IN THE BOOK

Composing (See Writing)

Comprehension
- classifying
- codes
- comparing and contrasting
- details

- drawing conclusions
- following directions
- main idea
- sequence of events

Creative Expression

Critical Thinking
- analyzing bait-and-switch advertisements
- analyzing cause and effect
- analyzing information
- classifying

- comparing and contrasting
- evaluating advertisements
- expressing opinions
- fact and opinion
- factual and persuasive writing

Drama (See also Nonverbal Communication)
- role playing

Grammar and Usage
- adjectives
- adverbs
- nouns

- proper nouns
- sentences
- verbs

Handwriting

Listening
- critical listening
- following directions

- listening for information

Literary Skills
- setting

Mechanics of Writing
- capitalization

- punctuation

Nonverbal Communication
- body language

- mime

Speaking
- doing commercials
- giving a report
- giving directions
- giving information
- interviewing

- making introductions
- ordering from a menu
- sharing experiences
- using the telephone

Spelling

Study Skills

- alphabetical order
- bar graphs
- catalogs
- charts
- classified ads
- diagrams
- dictionary
- flow charts
- index
- invoices
- job applications
- line graphs
- maps
- newspapers
- order forms
- schedules
- skimming
- taking notes
- telephone books
- surveys

Vocabulary

- abbreviations
- antonyms
- compound words
- content area words
- synonyms
- words from other languages

Word Recognition

- blends
- suffixes
- syllables
- vowel sounds

Writing

- advertisements
- autobiographical sketches
- business fliers
- business letters
- catalog copy
- cereal box labels
- codes
- commercials
- critiques
- dialogue
- directions
- essays
- friendly letters
- greeting cards
- invitations
- job descriptions
- lost and found notices
- menus
- messages
- news reports
- paragraphs
- phrases
- poems
- post cards
- product labels
- programs
- reports
- résumés
- sentences
- song lyrics
- summaries
- telegrams
- thank-you notes
- travel brochures

CURRICULAR AREAS RELATED TO ACTIVITIES

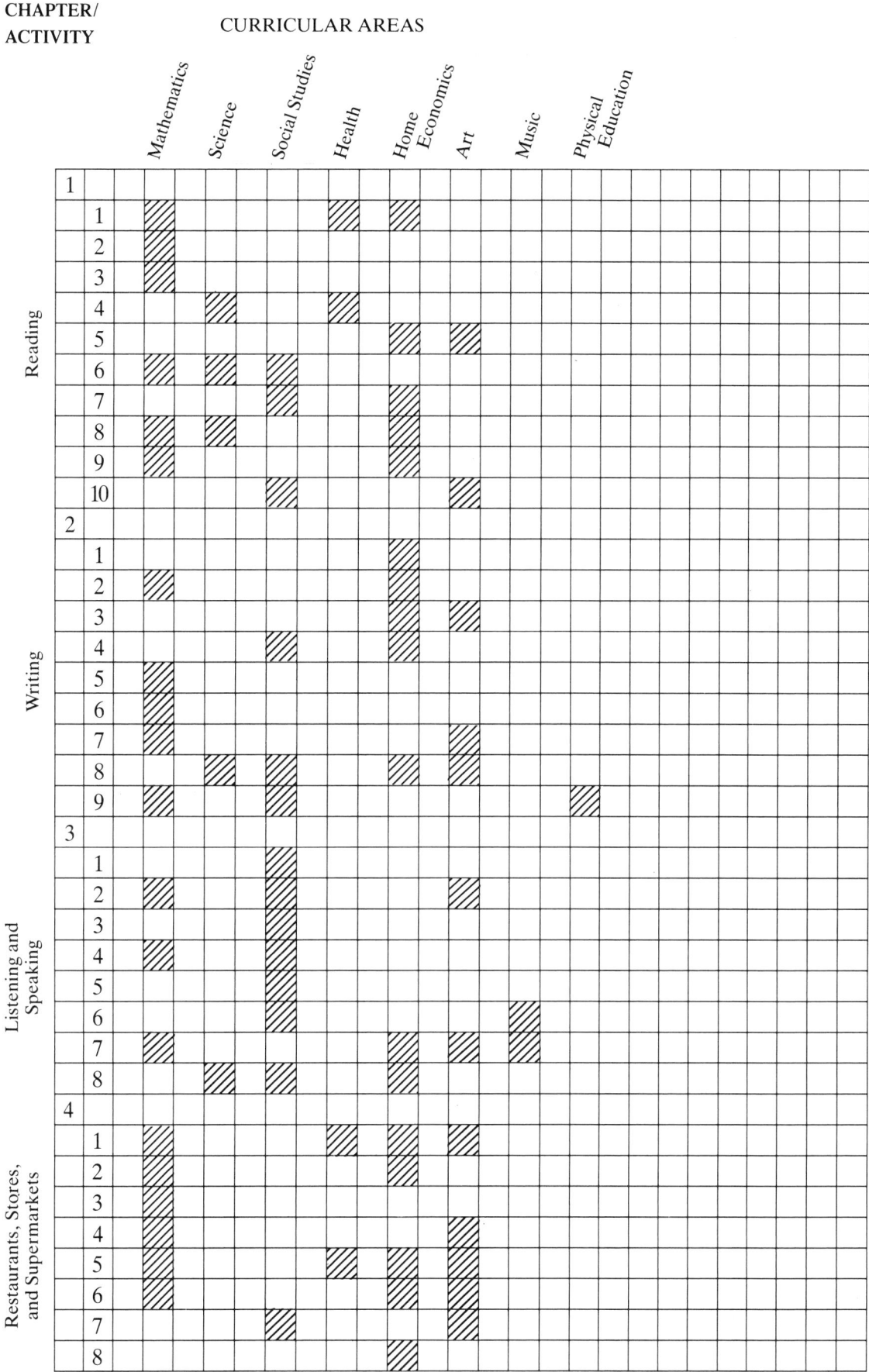

CURRICULAR AREAS RELATED TO ACTIVITIES

CHAPTER/ ACTIVITY CURRICULAR AREAS

Chapter / Activity	Mathematics	Science	Social Studies	Health	Home Economics	Art	Music	Physical Education
5								
Careers, Jobs, and Chores 1			▨					
2		▨	▨		▨	▨		
3			▨					
4			▨					
5			▨					
6			▨					
7			▨		▨	▨		
8	▨		▨		▨			
6								
Entertainment and Leisure Time 1						▨		
2								▨
3	▨							
4	▨					▨		▨
5	▨		▨			▨		
6	▨		▨					▨
7	▨							
7								
Holidays and Special Occasions 1			▨			▨		
2		▨				▨		
3	▨					▨		
4								▨
5	▨		▨		▨	▨		
6	▨			▨	▨			
8								
Projects 1	▨		▨			▨		
2			▨			▨		
3			▨			▨		
4			▨			▨		
5			▨			▨		
6	▨		▨			▨		

Introduction

No doubt about it—kids are consumers! They start at a very young age, progressing from the back seat of a shopping cart, through the back aisle of a toy store, to the back lot of an automobile dealership. And, throughout childhood, youngsters are bombarded with advertising—visual, written, and implied—and they are influenced by people—parents, peers, and television personalities. We need to help our children learn to sort through these messages and make their own wise and effective decisions. We believe that our students must learn to cooperate with each other in order to identify and solve problems and to make decisions in the real world.

The heart of real-world learning, of being a smart consumer, is critical thinking and problem solving. Within the educational community there's a growing emphasis on the importance of teaching these skills throughout the curriculum. And within the community at large, there's an expectation that schools should teach the survival skills needed to function successfully and responsibly in the real world.

This book is our response to these concerns. We have found that the best way to help kids learn to think critically and solve problems successfully is to have them participate in the real-life situations facing consumers. The activities in this book require students to make consumer decisions related to earning, saving, sharing, and spending money. And since consumer education is more than just decisions about money, they must also make decisions related to safety, health, and general well-being.

We realize that many of you are already putting a lot of effort into teaching real-world skills. The purpose of this book is to provide you with a rich collection of ideas and materials that will make it easier for you to do an even better job of making your reading and language arts curriculum "real"—with the big payoff, a growing "world" of wise consumers.

What You'll Find in This Book

A collection of real-world reading and language arts activities—and lots of learning excitement—is what you'll find in this book. These are not just straightforward reading or writing assignments; they are real-world learning experiences based on situations that we meet every day. But first, let's look at how the book is put together.

The Book's Organization

The activities are organized into two main categories—skills and consumer topics. In chapters 1, 2, and 3, the focus is on skill areas: Reading, Writing, and Listening and Speaking. The other activity chapters (4 through 7) focus on real-world reading and language arts applications—Restaurants, Stores, and Supermarkets; Careers, Jobs, and Chores; Entertainment and Leisure Time; Holidays and Special Occasions.

The last three chapters have quite a different flavor. Chapter 8, Projects, describes six comprehensive projects that are designed to give your students in-depth opportunities to apply their real-world reading and language arts skills! Chapter 9, Tips for Teachers, helps you plan the activities to suit your particular needs. Chapter 10, Materials and Resources, consists of suggestions and ideas for using the real-world materials (ads, cereal boxes, menus, travel brochures, and so on) that you'll find throughout the book.

Organization of the Activity Chapters

There are three parts to each of the activity chapters (Chapters 1 through 7). The first part is a page of introductory suggestions. On this page, we offer you some special thoughts about using the activities in the chapter.

The second part, which takes up the bulk of each chapter, is the collection of activities. Their format is described in detail on the next page.

The third part is at the end of each chapter, where you'll find a collection of Quick and Easy activities. These are five-minute fillers, the kind of activities that are perfect for those moments when it's too late to start a new lesson but too early to go to lunch!

Format of the Activities

All the activities are written in a simple, easy-to-use format. Each one starts on a new page and includes the following information:

The title tells the main idea of the activity.

Brief description of the activity.

The grade levels for which the activity is most appropriate.

Activity or project number.

Reading/Language Arts Skills: The reading or language arts skills used in the activity.

Curricular Areas: Other areas of the curriculum that are included in the content and/or process of the activity.

Materials: Items used in the activity.

A personal note with some of our thoughts about the activity.

PREPARATION: Things to be done before introducing the activity.

DISCUSSION: Discussion questions preceding the activity, to highlight the main ideas and concepts.

DIRECTIONS: Step-by-step instructions for directing the activity, written in the actual words you might want to use. (In parentheses are instructions meant only for you.)

VARIATIONS: Ideas for extending or varying the activity.

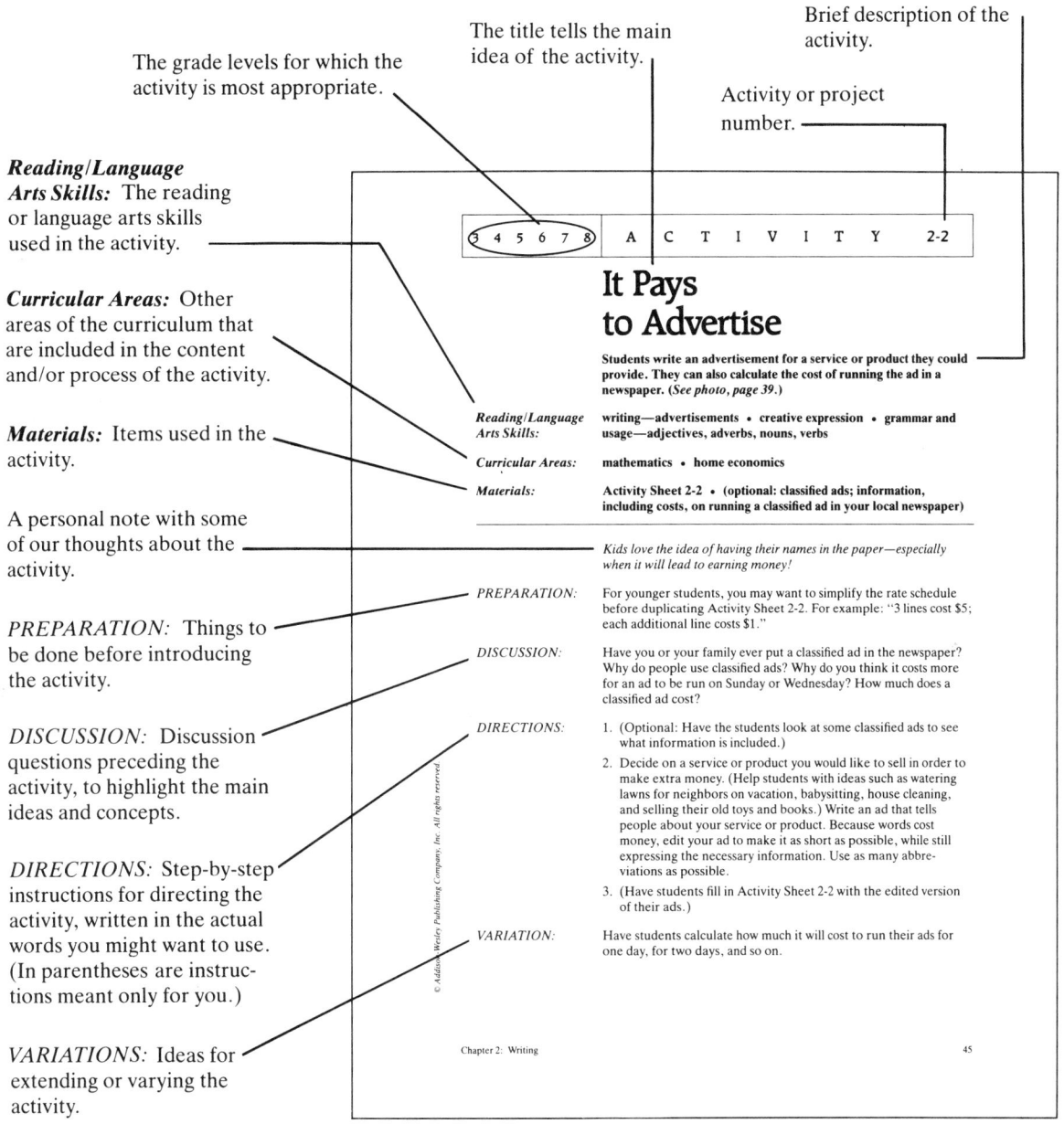

3 4 5 6 7 8   A C T I V I T Y   2-2

It Pays to Advertise

Students write an advertisement for a service or product they could provide. They can also calculate the cost of running the ad in a newspaper. (*See photo, page 39.*)

Reading/Language Arts Skills: writing—advertisements • creative expression • grammar and usage—adjectives, adverbs, nouns, verbs

Curricular Areas: mathematics • home economics

Materials: Activity Sheet 2-2 • (optional: classified ads; information, including costs, on running a classified ad in your local newspaper)

Kids love the idea of having their names in the paper—especially when it will lead to earning money!

PREPARATION: For younger students, you may want to simplify the rate schedule before duplicating Activity Sheet 2-2. For example: "3 lines cost $5; each additional line costs $1."

DISCUSSION: Have you or your family ever put a classified ad in the newspaper? Why do people use classified ads? Why do you think it costs more for an ad to be run on Sunday or Wednesday? How much does a classified ad cost?

DIRECTIONS:
1. (Optional: Have the students look at some classified ads to see what information is included.)
2. Decide on a service or product you would like to sell in order to make extra money. (Help students with ideas such as watering lawns for neighbors on vacation, babysitting, house cleaning, and selling their old toys and books.) Write an ad that tells people about your service or product. Because words cost money, edit your ad to make it as short as possible, while still expressing the necessary information. Use as many abbreviations as possible.
3. (Have students fill in Activity Sheet 2-2 with the edited version of their ads.)

VARIATION: Have students calculate how much it will cost to run their ads for one day, for two days, and so on.

Chapter 2: Writing   45

Underlying Themes

The main themes of this book are real-world problems and reading and language arts applications. Because these ideas are so closely related to the lives of real people, we've also emphasized two underlying themes that relate to the human aspect of the classroom.

One of these themes reflects our respect for the uniqueness of each child. Some activities are designed to encourage children to express their opinions, to name a favorite thing, or to describe something unique about themselves. In other activities, there are suggestions to help you create a warm, supportive environment for your students. And at the end of the book, you'll find award certificates for those occasions when you want to recognize something special about your students.

Our second underlying theme is promoting good relations among the school, the home, and the community. Because you're teaching about the real world, you'll find that parents and other members of the community will be especially interested in getting involved. For some lessons, you may want to call on them for information or materials; for other lessons, you may find it appropriate to invite them as observers or even participants. We hope you'll take advantage of these consumer-related opportunities for your students to interact with the adults in your community. The adults will love the chance to know more about what's going on at school; you'll end up with a strong, supportive group of people who'll be eager to help in any way they can; and your students will know that they live in a very special world!

Part 1.
Skill Area Activities

Reading

Reading Apple Wheat Crackles   Activity 1-1

1. *Reading Apple Wheat Crackles*

2. *An A to Z Activity*

3. *Index Treasure Hunt*

4. *Message on a Bottle*

5. *Abbreviated Ad Art*

6. *Monitoring Your Magazine*

7. *This Move Is Classified*

8. *A Twisted Memory Teaser*

9. *The Warranty Game*

10. *Sell Your Setting*

11. *Quick and Easy*

   A. *Keep Your Eyes on the Y's*
   B. *A-B-Seeds*
   C. *Vowels—Eat 'Em Up!*
   D. *Blend Spending*
   E. *Classy Syllables*
   F. *Where the Action Is*
   G. *Just the Facts, Please*

"New and improved!" "Refreshing and natural!" "Four out of five doctors recommend. . . ." Words, slogans, facts, and opinions! The consumer is constantly bombarded with written messages. Understanding—truly comprehending—these messages is essential to being an effective consumer.

People are at a disadvantage when they don't really comprehend what they are reading. Product labels, warranties, newspapers, and advertisements are full of written information. Not knowing the meaning of just one word or phrase all too often leads to unwise consumer decisions.

In this chapter, you'll find activities that use newspapers, catalogs, warranties, and a variety of other materials to focus on comprehension, critical thinking skills, and consumer vocabulary. The activities are easy to prepare, easy to explain, and exciting for the kids to do!

Naturally . . .
Four out of five teachers recommend the "new" and "improved" activities in this "refreshing" chapter!

Reading Apple Wheat Crackles

Students find factual and persuasive information on food packages and labels. (*See photo, page 3.*)

Reading/Language Arts Skills:	**comprehension—comparing and contrasting • critical thinking—factual and persuasive writing • vocabulary—content area words • writing—cereal box labels**
Curricular Areas:	**health • home economics • mathematics**
Materials:	**Activity Sheets 1-1a and 1-1b • cereal box front, back, and sides (pages 9, 10, and 11) • empty food boxes, bottles, and cans**

Start the day with a healthy breakfast cereal lesson! Add some fruitful discussion, pour on some encouragement, and top with some real cereal treats. Your class will eat it up!

PREPARATION:

1. Set up a collection of empty food containers in the classroom for this activity, or have students look in their kitchen cabinets at home to find the information they need.

2. Make copies of Activity Sheets 1-1a and 1-1b and the cereal box front, back, and sides. (If you like, run copies of the cereal box labels on colored paper, and have students color them with markers or crayons and paste them onto boxes to look like real cereal packages.)

3. Optional: Have students prepare "Crackling Party Mix" (recipe on page 11), using a cereal of their choice.

FACTUAL INFORMATION

A. Nutrition

DISCUSSION:

What does *nutrition* mean? (the food you eat and how your body uses it) What kind of nutrition information is included on the labels of food products? (calories per serving, percentage of U.S. recommended daily allowances of protein, vitamins, and minerals; amount of fat, carbohydrate, cholesterol, sodium, and so on) Where can we find this information on a cereal box? (usually on the side panels)

DIRECTIONS:

Pass a copy of the cereal box front, back, and sides to each student. (Have students complete Activity Sheet 1-1a.)

B. Ingredients

DISCUSSION: Are the ingredients always listed on a package? Are the ingredients on labels listed alphabetically? (no) In what order are they listed? (By percent of contents. The ingredient that makes up the greatest part of the product comes first. The next greatest comes second, and so on. The ingredient that there is the least of comes last.)

DIRECTIONS:
1. (Make sure that students have access to two or more packages of the same type of product. For example, two cereal boxes, soup cans, or bread wrappers.)
2. Which ingredient does each product have the most of? What is the second greatest ingredient? Which ingredient does each product have the least of? Did anything surprise you?
3. Let's compare the ingredients listed on our food packages. Make a list of items that are used in both products. Are there any ingredients listed on one label but not the other? Make a separate list of those ingredients.

PERSUASIVE INFORMATION

DISCUSSION: What does *persuade* mean? (to make someone believe something; to convince) Can you find examples of persuasive words or phrases on the Apple Wheat Crackles cereal box? ("Mom and Dad will be excited . . . ," "One bite will convince the whole family!" and so on) Where can you usually find this type of information on a cereal box? (on the front and back)

DIRECTIONS:
1. (Have students complete Activity Sheet 1-1b.)
2. Now, rewrite the information on the cereal box so that only factual information is presented.

Reading Apple Wheat Crackles

Factual Information: Nutrition

Nutrition—the food you eat and how your body uses it

Your job is to find nutrition words on food labels. Look for each nutrition word listed below on the side panels of the Apple Wheat Crackles box. Put a check mark next to each word you find. Do the same thing using labels from two other food products.

NUTRITION WORD	FOOD LABELS THAT USE THE WORD		
	1. Apple Wheat Crackles	2.	3.
1. Calories			
2. Protein			
3. Carbohydrate			
4. Fat			
5. Iron			
6. Calcium			
7. Phosphorus			
8. Magnesium			
9. Vitamins			
10. Riboflavin			
11. Niacin			
12. Thiamine			
13. Sodium			
14. Cholesterol			
15. Folic Acid			

Reading Apple Wheat Crackles
Persuasive Information

Persuade—to make someone believe
something; to convince

Your job is to find persuasive words or phrases on food labels. On the lines provided,
write the persuasive words or phrases that appear on the Apple Wheat Crackles box.
Do the same for two other food product labels. Circle any words that appear on more
than one label.

PERSUASIVE WORDS		
1. Apple Wheat Crackles	2.	3.

Cereal Box Front
(Use for Activities 1-1, 1-2, and 4-5.)

Cereal Box Back
(Use for Activities 1-1, 1-2, and 4-5.)

Now you can enjoy a cereal that is good for you and fun to eat!! Just pour on the milk and you can hear the tasty little flakes crackle with excitement as they mingle with chunks of dried apples. Mom and Dad will be excited, too, when they know that *Apple Wheat Crackles* is vitamin enriched, 100% wheat, and contains no sugar or salt. M-m-m! One bite will convince the whole family! So try the naturally sweet, crunchy taste of *Apple Wheat Crackles* today!

Easy-to-make yogurt topping and party mix recipes on side panel.

Cereal Box Side Panels
(Use for Activities 1-1, 1-2, and 4-5.)

INGREDIENTS: Whole Wheat, Wheat Bran, Dried Apples, Coconut Oil, Non-fat Dry Milk, Honey, Cinnamon, Natural Flavor.

NUTRITION INFORMATION PER SERVING

Serving size   1 oz. (28.3g)
Servings per container   16

CEREAL		WITH ½ CUP NONFAT MILK
Calories	110	155
Protein	3g	7g
Carbohydrate	20g	25g
Fat	3g	3g
Sodium	0mg	60mg
Potassium	10mg	210mg

PERCENTAGE OF U.S. RECOMMENDED DAILY ALLOWANCES (% U.S. RDA)

Protein	4	10
Vitamin A	10	12
Vitamin C	*	*
Thiamin	10	14
Riboflavin	8	20
Niacin	10	10
Calcium	2	15
Iron	5	5
Vitamin D	5	15

*Contains less than 2% of the U.S. RDA for this nutrient.

NATURAL YOGURT TOPPING

1 cup Apple Wheat Crackles cereal

¼ cup raisins

¼ cup sunflower seeds

¼ cup coconut (shredded)

1 tsp. cinnamon

Combine ingredients in a bowl. Toss until mixed. Sprinkle on top of your favorite flavored yogurt. Garnish with an apple slice. Topping for 12 yogurt servings.

CRACKLING PARTY MIX

2 cups Apple Wheat Crackles cereal

½ cup walnuts

½ cup peanuts

½ cup banana chips

½ cup sesame sticks

Put all ingredients into a bowl. Toss them until mixed. Makes 8 servings.

An *A* to *Z* Activity

Students count and record the total number of times each letter of the alphabet appears in each person's name. They predict and then verify how often letters occur on a cereal box and then in a reading passage. Discussion focuses on the consumer implications of how often certain letters occur in words.

Reading/Language Arts Skills: comprehension—comparing and contrasting, drawing conclusions

Curricular Areas: mathematics

Materials: **cereal box front, back, and sides (pages 9, 10, and 11) • books or magazines • (optional: stick-on labels and a Scrabble® game)**

This activity is as easy as A, B, Z!

A. *An activity for the N-tire class*

B. *An E-Z cereal box activity*

Z. *An activity that X-tends learning*

PREPARATION: On the chalkboard list the letters of the alphabet from *A* to *Z*. Meanwhile, have each student list the letters on a piece of paper.

DISCUSSION: Which letters on a typewriter do you think would wear out first? In a Scrabble® game, which letters do you think you get most often? Which do you get least often? If you wanted to sell a package of stick-on alphabet letters that people could use to decorate and label their belongings, how many of each letter would you include?

DIRECTIONS: A. An Activity for the N-tire Class

1. On your list of alphabet letters (see *PREPARATION*), circle the two letters you think will appear *most* often in people's names. Put a triangle around one that you think might not appear at all. Put a square around the two letters you think will appear *least* often.

2. Print your first and last name at the top of the page. On your alphabet list, put one tally mark next to each letter that appears in your name. If a letter appears twice in your name, you'll need two marks next to that letter.

3. Let's combine our tally marks. Will the people at this table (or in this row) please transfer their tally marks to the alphabet on the chalkboard. (Continue until all students have been to the chalkboard.)

4. Which letters appear *most* often? Which appear *least* often? Which do not appear at all?

5. Do you think we'd get a similar result if we tallied the letters in the names of the students in the class across the hall? What do the results imply if you want to package and sell sets of stick-on letters to be used to label belongings? Would you leave out any letters?

B. An E-Z Cereal Box Activity

1. (Students may work in pairs. Pass a copy of the cereal box front, back, and sides to each student or pair of students.)

2. On a piece of paper, list the letters of the alphabet from *A* to *Z*. Circle the two letters you think will appear *most* often on the cereal box. Put a square around the two letters you think will appear *least* often. Put a triangle around one letter you think will not appear at all.

3. Read the advertisement on the back of the Apple Wheat Crackles cereal box that begins: "Now you can enjoy . . ." and ends ". . . Apple Wheat Crackles today!"

4. Count the number of times the letter *A* appears in the passage. Record your answer next to the letter *A* on your paper. Continue counting and recording each letter of the alphabet. (Answers: *A* 33, *B* 2, *C* 17, *D* 10, *E* 40, *F* 4, *G* 3, *H* 19, *I* 19, *J* 2, *K* 6, *L* 19, *M* 10, *N* 25, *O* 25, *P* 7, *Q* 0, *R* 11, *S* 14, *T* 35, *U* 10, *V* 2, *W* 12, *X* 0, *Y* 11, *Z* 0)

5. Look back at the letters around which you put a circle, a square, and a triangle. Compare your predictions with your actual count.

6. Count and record the number of times each letter appears on the front of the box. Do they appear with the same frequency? (Answers: *A* 20, *B* 1, *C* 6, *D* 10, *E* 20, *F* 3, *G* 3, *H* 8, *I* 15, *J* 0, *K* 3, *L* 13, *M* 4, *N* 17, *O* 14, *P* 11, *Q* 0, *R* 11, *S* 9, *T* 12, *U* 4, *V* 2, *W* 7, *X* 0, *Y* 0, *Z* 1) Did the same letters appear most frequently on both the front and back? (Yes; *A* and *E* were most frequent on both.) Were there letters that did not appear on either the front or back? (Yes; *Q* and *X*.)

Z. An Activity that X-tends Learning

1. Choose a paragraph of at least fifty words from a book or a magazine. List the letters of the alphabet on a piece of paper. Count and record each letter of the alphabet as it appears in the paragraph. Compare your results with the cereal box results.

2. Do you think the letter frequency is different on menus or on record albums? How could you find out?

Index
Treasure Hunt

One student describes an item in a catalog and the others use the index to find the item's page and catalog number.

Reading/Language Arts Skills: **comprehension—details, following directions • study skills— index, catalogs • listening—listening for information • speaking—giving information**

Curricular Areas: **mathematics**

Materials: **a classroom set of the *same* catalog (They're easy to get—look at page 258 for help.)**

After just one Index Treasure Hunt, students will be eager to do it again . . . and again . . . and again!

DISCUSSION: What is an index? Where is an index found? Why is it useful? How is information listed?

DIRECTIONS: 1. (To introduce the Index Treasure Hunt, describe an item and the page it is on in the catalog. Ask students to find the item and name its catalog number.) I'm on a treasure hunt on page 17 and have found a red wool sweater. What is its catalog number?

2. (Next, have students locate the item in the index.) In the index, where would this item be listed? (under "Sweaters") Turn to the index. What are the pages for sweaters?

3. (For the next treasure hunt, describe an item and then ask students to find the page it is on *and* the catalog number.) My treasure is a white plastic desk with three drawers on the right side and a matching chair. What page is it on? What is its catalog number?

4. (Repeat the activity several times. Students can take turns leading the treasure hunt.)

VARIATION: Have students work in pairs or small groups. Have one student describe the item and the other students find the page and catalog number.

Message on a Bottle

Students read bottle labels to find warnings and other important information.

Reading/Language Arts Skills:	**comprehension—main idea and details, drawing conclusions • critical thinking—analyzing information**
Curricular Areas:	**health • science**
Materials:	**Activity Sheet 1-4 • (optional: empty medicine, vitamin, or other bottles with warnings on their labels. Be sure that all contents have been removed and that the bottles have been thoroughly washed.)**

Notice: Smart consumers have determined that reading labels may be beneficial to your health!

DISCUSSION: What types of bottles contain warning messages on their labels? (medicines, vitamins, cleaning fluids, insecticides) Why is it important to read the labels before using these products? (Labels give directions for safe use, proper dosage, and antidotes.)

DIRECTIONS: (Have students complete Activity Sheet 1-4.)

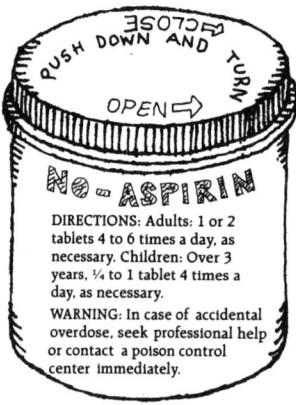

Message on a Bottle

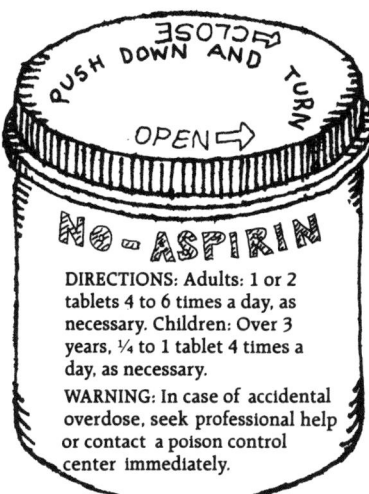

NO-ASPIRIN

1. What should be done in case of accidental overdose?

   _____

2. What is the adult dosage of No-Aspirin? _____

   _____

3. How often may an adult take a tablet? _____

   _____

4. What is the children's dosage? _____

   _____

MIGHTY-VIT

1. Would Mighty-Vit be a good vitamin choice for someone on a

   salt-free diet? _____ Why or why not?

   _____

2. What is the expiration date on this bottle? _____

3. Is this product suitable for children under 4 years old? _____

   How do you know? _____

   _____

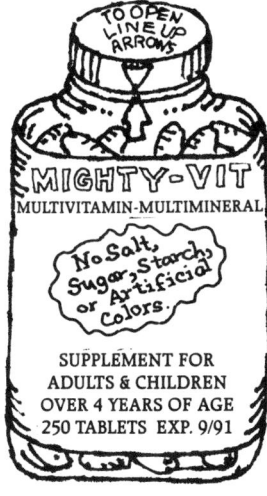

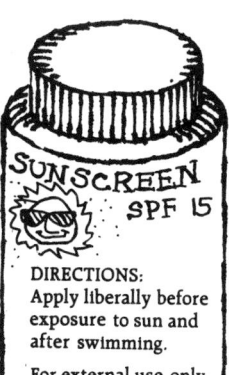

SUNSCREEN

1. Suppose you broke out in a rash after using this sunscreen.

   What should you do? _____

   _____

2. When should this sunscreen be applied? _____

   _____

3. Where should you avoid applying this product? _____

   _____

Abbreviated Ad Art

Students find abbreviations in the classified ads, then make posters showing common abbreviations in various types of ads.

Reading/Language Arts Skills: **comprehension—comparing and contrasting • vocabulary— abbreviations, content area words • study skills—newspapers, skimming • writing—advertisements • spelling**

Curricular Areas: **art • home economics**

Materials: **classified ads section of the newspaper for each student • poster paper • crayons or markers • scissors • paste, tape, or staplers**

This activity will "add" an instant (and not so "abbreviated!") bulletin board to your room.

DISCUSSION: What is an abbreviation? Why would someone want to use an abbreviation in an ad? Why is it important to be able to decipher abbreviations? Do you think an automobile ad uses the same abbreviations as a real estate ad?

DIRECTIONS:

1. Please skim your classified ads and look for abbreviations. Circle the abbreviations with your crayon or marker.

2. What are some of the abbreviations you found? What are their meanings? (List students' abbreviations and meanings on the chalkboard.)

3. We're going to make posters to illustrate common abbreviations used in various types of ads. Please divide your poster paper into four sections. Label each section with one type of classified ad in your paper (automobiles, computers, employment, lost and found, real estate, video equipment, and so on).

4. Now search each type of ad for common abbreviations. Cut the ads out and paste them in the correct section on your poster. Below each ad, write the abbreviations used and their meanings (example: *Automobile Ads*—a.c. = air conditioning, t.o.p. = take over payments).

5. Decorate your posters by drawing a car, a house, dollar signs, and so on in proper sections of the poster.

6. (After posters are finished:) Let's compare posters. What are some of the most common abbreviations used in real estate (lost and found, employment) ads? What is the most interesting information you've included on your posters?

VARIATION: Have students write classified ads using abbreviations (sell the principal's car, buy a new desk, find a lost book, and so on).

Monitoring Your Magazine

Over a period of several months, students keep an eye on a favorite feature in a monthly magazine to find out how that feature varies from month to month.

Reading/Language Arts Skills: **comprehension—main idea, comparing and contrasting • critical thinking—expressing opinions • writing—summaries • listening—listening for information • speaking—giving a report**

Curricular Areas: **social studies • science • mathematics**

Materials: **at least one monthly magazine for students (Many school libraries subscribe to magazines such as *Penny Power, Weekly Reader, Ranger Rick, Ebony Jr.,* or *Cricket*.)**

Your students will become literary critics as they follow favorite features in monthly magazines.

PREPARATION: Display several copies of the magazines you'll be using.

DISCUSSION: Who is familiar with this magazine? What is your favorite regular feature? Why?

DIRECTIONS:
1. For the next several months, we're going to read carefully a regular feature of this magazine. This week, I want each of you to look through at least two past issues of this magazine and decide which feature you would enjoy reading each month.

2. (The following week, after students have had time to complete the above assignment:) Let's talk about our favorite features in the magazine. (Call on different students.) What is your favorite? Why?

3. In what ways would you expect this feature to be the same every month? (format, author, topic) How might it differ from month to month?

4. On a piece of paper, please write your name and the feature you plan to read each month.

5. Each time a new issue arrives, please read the feature you've chosen and then write a summary of it. Include the title, the author, and the main idea(s). After you've read this feature in at least four issues of the magazine, please review your four summaries and compare them. Be ready to tell the class how this magazine feature was the same as well as how it differed from month to month.

6. (After students have read at least four issues, have them prepare their summary reports. Have five or six students sign up for each day of the week to give their reports to the class. If several students have been reading the same feature, you may want to have them do their reports on the same day.)

7. Now we're ready to hear from those who have been reading (name a feature) every month. Please tell us how the feature varied from month to month. (Encourage questions and responses from the rest of the class.)

8. Why do magazines have certain features that are included in every issue? Are there any features that you would like to add to this magazine? Are there any you would discontinue?

This Move Is Classified

Students use the classified ads to locate items or to hire workers needed when moving from one home to another.

Reading/Language Arts Skills: comprehension—classifying • study skills—newspapers, classified ads

Curricular Areas: social studies • home economics

Materials: Activity Sheet 1-7 • classified ads for each student • scissors • paste, tape, or staplers

---

In our transient society, many students move several times during their school careers. Here's a chance to have your class look more closely at some of the details involved in moving.

PREPARATION: Make a copy of Activity Sheet 1-7 and fill in appropriate prices. Duplicate the Activity Sheet for each student.

DISCUSSION: Who in our class moved here after school began? (Encourage those students to share their experiences.) If your family decided to move from where you presently live to a larger place, what are some of the things you might have to do? (Locate a new house or apartment, find a mover, hire someone to weed your new yard and trim hedges, and, perhaps, buy more furniture or appliances.) What section of the newspaper could help you with some of these jobs? (the classified section)

DIRECTIONS: (Give each student a classified ads section, and have them complete Activity Sheet 1-7.)

VARIATION: On another day, have students work cooperatively in groups to identify five situations that require hiring someone or purchasing items found in the classified ads. They can then design their own worksheets, similar to Activity Sheet 1-7, to be used on another day.

This Move is Classified

Read each situation below. Then look through your classified ads and locate at least one ad for each situation, cut it out, and paste it in the proper section below.

C L A S S I F I E D

Real Estate

1. Your family would like to rent a three-bedroom house. You have a pet dog.

Automobiles

2. Your mother needs a reliable used car for under $ _____ .

Household Goods

3. Your old place had only two bedrooms. You need furniture for the third bedroom.

Sporting Goods

4. You need a bike to ride to school. Find a used ten-speed for under $ _____ .

Services Offered

5. Your new yard is overgrown with weeds. You need a gardener to help get it in shape.

A Twisted Memory Teaser

Students read a recipe for soft pretzels and then try to recall as many words and numbers as possible.

Reading/Language Arts Skills: **comprehension—details, following directions • listening—listening for information**

Curricular Areas: **home economics • science • mathematics**

Materials: **recipe for soft pretzels (page 27) • (optional: ingredients and utensils to prepare soft pretzels—see page 27)**

This activity is sure to put a new "twist" on learning—and your students will love it!

DIRECTIONS:

1. (Give each student a copy of the recipe for soft pretzels turned face down on the desks.) After you read this recipe, I'll ask each of you to see how much information you can recall without looking back at the recipe.

2. Please turn your papers over and read and study the recipe for two minutes. (Two minutes later:) Now turn your papers face down on your desks.

3. On a separate piece of paper write all the ingredients from the recipe that you can recall. You have three minutes to do this.

4. Now, I'll read the recipe and you check your paper to see how many ingredients you recalled.

VARIATIONS:

1. Students can actually prepare soft pretzels in class, with a slight twist! (Note: Parents are often willing to pick up the dough, bake it in their ovens at home, and return the warm, tasty pretzels to the classroom for a treat worth writing about!)

2. Place all the ingredients and utensils, except one, on a table. Have students read the recipe and decide whether all the ingredients and utensils are on the table. Ask, "Is everything here that we need? What is missing?" When the correct response is given, place the missing item on the table.

3. Have students take turns reading the recipe directions as you prepare the pretzel dough. Once the dough has risen, divide it among students so that they can form their own pretzel shapes on small pieces of foil. (Or, divide students into small groups and allow them to make their own pretzel dough.)

Soft Pretzels

Here's a favorite recipe that's been shared from school to school and adapted along the way. We now share it with you.

Ingredients:

1 cake yeast

1½ cups warm water

1 tsp salt

2 tbsp honey

4 cups sifted whole-wheat flour

1 large egg, beaten

coarse salt (optional)

Utensils:

mixing bowl

flour sifter

egg beater or fork

measuring cup and spoons

rolling pin

knife

pastry brush

cookie sheet

dish towel

foil

oven or toaster oven

Dissolve yeast in warm water. Add salt and honey. Blend in flour. Place dough on a floured breadboard or counter and knead until smooth. Form the dough into a ball and put it back in the bowl. Cover with a dish towel and leave in a warm, dark place until the dough has doubled in size (about 30 minutes).

Roll the dough out on a floured surface and cut into strips. Form each strip into a knot. Place on a well-greased cookie sheet. Brush pretzels with beaten egg and sprinkle lightly with coarse salt (optional). Bake immediately at 425° for 12–15 minutes or until lightly browned.

The Warranty Game

Students play a game designed to help them realize that making a warranty work for the consumer often requires very careful reading.

Reading/Language Arts Skills: **comprehension—details, following directions • critical thinking—analyzing cause and effect**

Curricular Areas: **mathematics • home economics**

Materials: **game board (page 277) • game spinner (page 276) • paper clip • pencil • Warranty Cards and Situation Cards (pages 31 and 32) • playing piece for each student (a coin, ring, or bean) • (optional: sample warranties for common purchases such as appliances and sports equipment)**

This game warrants your students' attention—we guarantee it!

PREPARATION: To make spinner:

1. Duplicate a game spinner (page 276) for each group of players.
2. Fill in the five sections with the numbers 1,2,3,4,5.

To make game board:

1. Duplicate a game board (page 277). You or your students can fill in the following information on the game board.

   A. Fill in each space with the numbers 1 through 26 followed by the word *month* or *months*.

   B. Randomly, fill in 12 spaces with:

   - Sole comes off shoe
   - Bicycle tire blows out
   - Clock spring breaks
   - Radio cord frays
   - Blow dryer catches on fire
   - Skateboard breaks in half
   - Computer monitor blows up
   - Arm falls off robot
   - Backpack zipper breaks
   - Baseball mitt unlaces
   - Bike lock won't shut
   - Microscope does not focus

C. You may want to sketch a picture of each situation on the game board (see illustration).

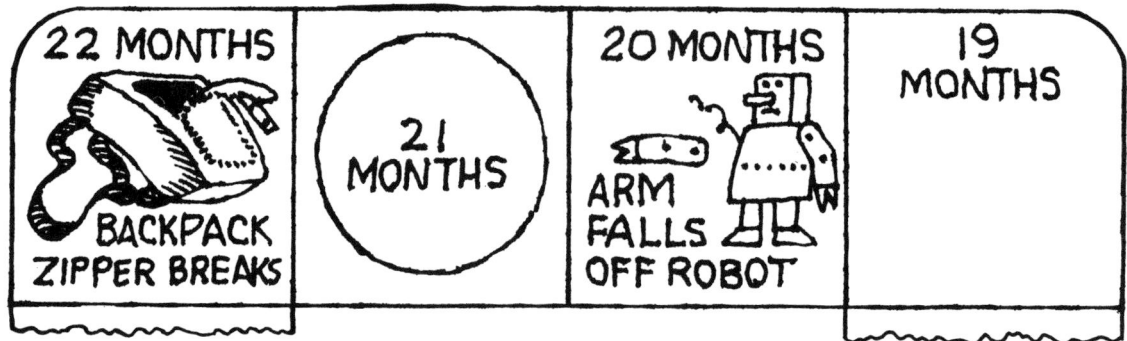

2. Duplicate a copy of the completed game board for each group of players. (Larger boards can be made by making a transparency and tracing around the projected game board on tag board or stiffening fabric used for interfacing.)

To make game cards:

1. Duplicate one set of Warranty and Situation Cards for each group of players.

2. Cut the cards apart. Mix them together and place them in a pile face down.

DIRECTIONS: (two to three players)

1. Players spin to determine which player will go first. The player with the highest spin starts the game. Play continues to the left.

2. Players begin by placing markers on the space marked *START*. They take turns spinning and move ahead the number of spaces indicated on the spinner.

3. If a player lands on a space with a product problem on it, he or she draws a card.

4. If the card picked is a Warranty Card, the player checks the space his or her marker is on to determine whether the warranty is still valid. If it is, the player spins again; if not, the player loses a turn.

5. If the card picked is a Situation Card, the player reads and follows the directions on the card.

6. Play continues until one player reaches the space marked *FINISH*.

SITUATION

You bought the bargain brand. No warranty. Move back 3 spaces.

SITUATION

You forgot to mail in the purchase verification card, so the warranty is not registered. Lose next turn.

SITUATION

The product has a lifetime warranty! Spin again.

SITUATION

You saved your receipt and the warranty covers all damage. Spin again.

SITUATION

The manufacturing company went out of business. Warranty is no longer valid. Move back 3 spaces.

SITUATION

Damage due to your misuse of the product. Move back 2 spaces.

SITUATION

You threw away your receipt. Warranty is no good without proof of purchase. Move back 4 spaces.

SITUATION

Product has a defective part that is covered by the warranty. Spin again.

SITUATION

Your warranty includes a 6-month service check of the product. Move ahead 2 spaces.

Sell Your Setting

Students design travel brochures describing the setting of a book or story they have read.

Reading/Language Arts Skills:	**literary skills: setting • creative expression • writing—travel brochures, post cards • spelling • handwriting**
Curricular Areas:	**art • social studies**
Materials:	**drawing paper • crayons or markers • sample travel brochure (pages 35 and 36) • (optional: travel brochures collected from a local travel agency • index cards)**

Students will enjoy this appealing alternative to book reports.

PREPARATION: (Optional: Make a copy of the sample brochure on pages 35 and 36 for each student. Copy the two pages back to back so that students can fold the single sheet of paper into a brochure.)

DISCUSSION: What is the *setting* of a story? Think about the setting of a story you have just read or of a favorite story. If you were a travel agent, how would you describe the setting? What activities might be available to a tourist there? (Distribute the sample travel brochure on pages 35 and 36 and have students fold it in thirds and then read it.) What information is included in this travel brochure?

DIRECTIONS: Create a travel brochure for the setting of your story. Include the following things:

A. Drawings and descriptions of places of interest

B. Special tours and side trips, and their cost and duration

C. Prices for meals, hotels, and so on

D. Where to write for information

Be creative! Design a brochure that will really motivate someone to travel to your setting by reading the book.

VARIATIONS:
1. Encourage students to compose their travel brochure descriptions on a word processor. They could also use a computer graphics program to create their brochure design.
2. Distribute index cards and have students design one or more postcards that show a scene from the story they read. Tell them to write a note to a friend on the back of the card telling about one of the exciting events that took place in the story. Encourage them to write as if they were actually there. Then tell them to address the postcard and design a stamp for the upper right-hand corner.

LODGING

CASTLE ON THE HILL

- Be treated like royalty
- Beautiful courtyard with wishing well
- Room service available

- Single occupancy: $125 per night

DWARFS' COTTAGES

- Must help with cooking and cleaning
- Must put up with occasional sneezing, snoring, and grumpiness
- Share room with 7 others

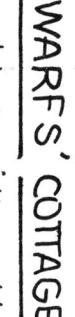

$15 per night

RESTAURANTS IN THE AREA

THE GARDEN OF EATIN'

Especially noted for its heavenly apple desserts

SAND-WITCH DELI

Ask about the stew-of-the-day!

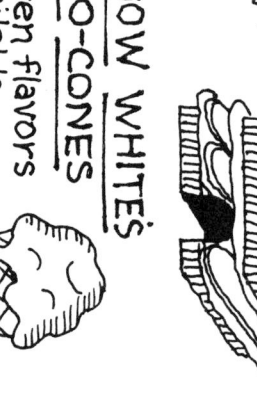

SNOW WHITE'S SNO-CONES

Seven flavors available

WAL-DWARF SALAD BAR

Specializing in mini salads for light eaters

SIDE TRIPS AVAILABLE

JEWEL MINE TOURS

Daily Mon.-Fri. 10 a.m.-12 noon
1 p.m.-3 p.m.

Sat. and Sun. 12 noon-2 p.m.

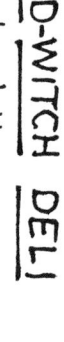

Adults: $2.00   Under 12: $1.00

APPLE MUSEUM

Special Display
Famous Poison Apple

Open daily   10 a.m.-4 p.m.
Admission: 50¢

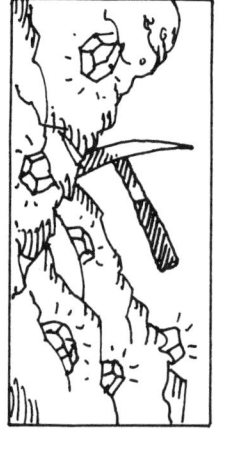

Quick and Easy

A. KEEP YOUR EYES ON THE *Y*'S

1. (List on the chalkboard:)

   buttery   spicy
   cheesy   minty
   fruity   nutty

2. What can be described with these adjectives? (food products) Do the products really contain these ingredients? How could you find out? (Check the list of ingredients on the label.) What does the -*y* ending really mean? ("somewhat like" or "full of")

3. (On another day, discuss other descriptive words or phrases that suggest a desirable quality, such as "real fruit flavor.") Does this phrase mean that there is real fruit in the food or that it only tastes like real fruit? How can you tell? (Read the label.)

B. A-B-SEEDS

1. Imagine that you work at a nursery. You have decided to arrange your flower seed packages in alphabetical order on the display rack so that customers can locate the seeds they want quickly. Put these seeds in alphabetical order.

Marigold	Wildflower Mix
Sweetpea	Aster
Nasturtium	Sweet Alyssum
Sweet William	Poppy
Pansy	Peony

2. (With the help of the class, list on the chalkboard words in a given category such as types of soup, spices, breakfast cereals, canned vegetables, and yogurt flavors. Have students arrange them alphabetically.)

C. VOWELS—EAT 'EM UP!

1. (On the chalkboard make headings of short vowels and have students make the same headings on lined paper, leaving enough space between each one so that words can be written under each heading.)

2. Look at the vowels as we say the short sound that each one makes. Now think of foods or beverages that contain that sound. Write as many as you can think of under each vowel heading (for example: apple, egg, spinach, hot dog, ketchup).

3. Now let's make a class list on the chalkboard. (Have students contribute several responses under each vowel as you write them down.) Do all of these things have the sound of (ă)?

D. BLEND SPENDING

1. (Write a two-letter blend on the chalkboard—for example, *st*.) Let's make a list of things we could buy at the supermarket that start with the blend *st*. (starch, steak, stewed tomatoes, stove-top stuffing, and so on)

2. (Repeat the activity using other blends: *br, sl, tr, cl, bl*, and so on.)

E. CLASSY SYLLABLES

1. Imagine that we have a new classroom but no supplies or equipment. Your job is to make a list of things we need to buy for our new room. The tricky part is that the list of things can only contain one-syllable words!

2. Brainstorm with a friend. Write as many one-syllable words as you can for classroom equipment and supplies.

3. Who would like to share their list? Please read it.

4. (Variation: Repeat the activity with two-syllable words and three-syllable words.)

F. WHERE THE ACTION IS

1. (Pass out articles from the newspaper to the class.) Please circle all the action verbs in the article you have.

2. (Call on one student.) How many action verbs did you find? Explain what the article is about and then read your circled action verbs to the class.

3. Why do you think some articles have more action verbs than others?

G. JUST THE FACTS, PLEASE

1. (Pass out newspaper or magazine advertisements to the class.) Please list only the facts stated in the ad.

2. Make a list of opinions expressed in the ad.

3. (Variation for older students: Repeat the activity with an editorial or letter to the editor from the newspaper.) Divide your writing paper in half. In one column, list the facts stated in the editorial or letter. In the other, list the opinions expressed.

Writing

It Pays to Advertise   Activity 2-2

1. *Ad-Libs*
2. *It Pays to Advertise*
3. *Create-a-Catalog*
4. *To Whom It May Concern*
5. *For a Code, Take Lemon Syrup*
6. *Dial M-Y P-H-O-N-E Number*
7. *A Classy Phone Book*
8. *Name That Word!*
9. *Walk Softly and Carry a Sharp Pencil*

10. *Quick and Easy*
   A. *Shopping List*
   B. *Food for Thought*
   C. *A Chalkboard Collage of Feelings*
   D. *Story Stretch*
   E. *Compose Yourself*
   F. *Brand Name Words*
   G. *Supermarket Anagrams*
   H. *Lost and Found*
   I. *The Mail Must Go Through*

C H A P T E R 2

"Let me do it! Let me do it!" This is a phrase we hear again and again as children eagerly try out new skills in their everyday lives. Whether it be painting, dialing the phone, stirring cake batter, wrapping a package, working with a computer, or any number of other activities, the plea is the same—"Let me do it!"

The activities in this chapter encourage the "I can do it" spirit while your students try out their writing skills in real-life situations. They learn the power of a well-written business letter and the value of being able to express themselves in clear, concise writing. The activities require that students form opinions, defend choices, and think critically—skills that are essential for consumers of all ages.

Students are also challenged to think clearly and creatively as they describe items to "Create-a-Catalog," write advertising copy, and design "A Classy Phone Book."

The ideas in this chapter, along with your creative efforts, provide a winning combination for introducing your students to the fun and challenge of real-life writing. "You can do it!"

Ad-Libs

Students place—and replace—the adjectives (or nouns, verbs, adverbs) in advertisements.

Reading/Language Arts Skills: **writing—advertisements • creative expression • grammar and usage—adjectives, adverbs, nouns, verbs**

Curricular Areas: **home economics**

Materials: **Activity Sheet 2-1 • (optional: magazine advertisements)**

After all those hours you've spent making carefully designed lesson plans, you'll love this chance to just "Ad-Lib" a lesson!

DISCUSSION:

1. (Write this sentence on the board:)

   This _____ cereal is for everyone.

   What word would make sense in the blank? Who can name another word that makes sense in the blank? What other words would also fit? What do we call the kind of words we've just listed? (adjectives)

2. (Write a second sentence on the board:)

   That cereal is _____.

   Let's name some single words that would fit in the blank. (When students begin to name words that were also on the first list, have them try out all the words from that list.) Would all the words on our first list make sense in this second sentence? What is the name we use for the kind of word that describes something? (adjective)

DIRECTIONS:

1. I have an ad for a secret product—but all the adjectives are missing! Please help me by giving me eight adjectives that I can use in my ad.

2. (As students suggest them, write the eight adjectives on the chalkboard.)

3. (Pass a copy of Activity Sheet 2-1 to each student.) Follow the directions on the sheet.

4. (After students have completed the Activity Sheet:) Now I want each of you to write an ad with at least eight blanks for adjectives. Choose a common product such as soap, cereal, shoes, or suitcases.

5. (Arrange students in pairs.) Tell your partner how many adjectives you need—but don't tell anything else about your ad!

6. Number your paper for the number of adjectives your partner needs, then make a list of adjectives. Give your list to your partner. Take turns reading your ads using an adjective from your partner's list each time you come to one of the blanks in your original ad.

VARIATIONS:

1. Follow the same procedure using real magazine advertisements. How do the new adjectives change the message? How does the ad sound if the adjectives are left out altogether?

2. Follow the same procedure to explore the functions of adverbs, nouns, or verbs.

Ad-Libs

1. Use the eight words listed on the chalkboard to fill in the empty spaces in the following advertisement.

   Next time you're in The _____ Supermarket,

   be sure to pick up a bunch of _____ carrots.

   Sandy's _____ carrots are always _____

   and _____. Your _____ family

   will enjoy the _____ taste of this

   _____ food.

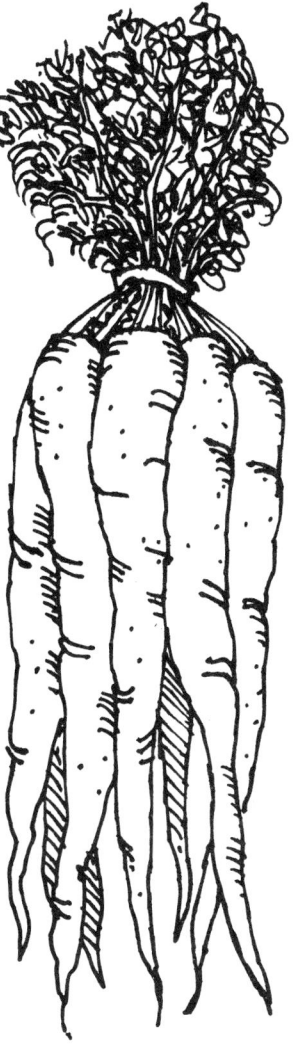

2. Replace the adjectives that don't make sense in the ad above with adjectives that do. Leave the adjectives that do make sense where they are.

   Next time you're in The _____ Supermarket,

   be sure to pick up a bunch of _____ carrots.

   Sandy's _____ carrots are always _____

   and _____. Your _____ family

   will enjoy the _____ taste of this

   _____ food.

3. Now be creative! Fill in the blanks with the best adjectives you can think of to sell the product.

   Next time you're in The _____ Supermarket,

   be sure to pick up a bunch of _____ carrots.

   Sandy's _____ carrots are always _____

   and _____. Your _____ family

   will enjoy the _____ taste of this

   _____ food.

It Pays to Advertise

Students write an advertisement for a service or product they could provide. They can also calculate the cost of running the ad in a newspaper. (*See photo, page 39.*)

Reading/Language Arts Skills:	**writing—advertisements • creative expression • spelling • study skills—newspapers • vocabulary—abbreviations**
Curricular Areas:	**mathematics • home economics**
Materials:	**Activity Sheet 2-2 • (optional: classified ads; information, including costs, on running a classified ad in your local newspaper)**

Kids love the idea of having their names in the paper—especially when it will lead to earning money!

PREPARATION: For younger students, you may want to simplify the rate schedule before duplicating Activity Sheet 2-2. For example: "3 lines cost $5; each additional line costs $1."

DISCUSSION: Have you or your family ever put a classified ad in the newspaper? Why do people use classified ads? Why do you think it costs more for an ad to be run on Sunday or Wednesday? How much does a classified ad cost?

DIRECTIONS:
1. (Optional: Have the students look at some classified ads to see what information is included.)

2. Decide on a service or product you would like to sell in order to make extra money. (Help students with ideas such as watering lawns for neighbors on vacation, babysitting, house cleaning, and selling their old toys and books.) Write an ad that tells people about your service or product. Because words cost money, edit your ad to make it as short as possible, while still expressing the necessary information. Use as many abbreviations as possible.

3. (Have students fill in Activity Sheet 2-2 with the edited version of their ads.)

VARIATION: Have students calculate how much it will cost to run their ads for one day, for two days, and so on.

It Pays to Advertise

Use this form to write your ad. There are 26 spaces per line. Each letter, number, punctuation mark, and space in your ad counts as one space. 3-line minimum, please.

	1	2	3	4	5	6	7	8	9	10	11	12	13	14	15	16	17	18	19	20	21	22	23	24	25	26
1 line																										
2 lines																										
3 lines																										
4 lines																										
5 lines																										
6 lines																										
7 lines																										
8 lines																										
9 lines																										
10 lines																										
11 lines																										
12 lines																										

How many days will the ad run? _____

List the days the ad will run. _____

3 LINES FOR 1 DAY—$6.00

Add $2.00 for each additional line.
Add $1.00 for each additional day.
Add $.50 extra for Wednesday or Sunday ads.

Create-a-Catalog

Students make their own catalogs. They design the cover, page layouts, and order form.

Reading/Language Arts Skills: **writing—catalog copy, dialogue • creative expression • handwriting • spelling**

Curricular Areas: **art • home economics**

Materials: **old catalogs • paper • scissors • paste or tape**

This activity will fill your room with happy and interested kids. They'll learn about catalogs—inside and out!

PREPARATION: Ask students to bring old catalogs to school. Magazines and ads will work, too. A sample letter to ask families for catalogs is included on page 251.

DISCUSSION: Suppose you were going into the mail-order business. What kinds of items would you like to sell? (bicycles, computers, clothing, and so on)

DIRECTIONS:

1. You're going to design a catalog that includes at least three categories of merchandise—such as toys, clothing, furniture, pet supplies, sports equipment—with at least six items in each category.

2. Think of the three categories you're going to use. Draw or cut out pictures of items you want to include in each category.

3. Fold blank paper in half to make catalog pages. Paste or tape pictures onto the blank pages. Leave plenty of space on each page for information about the items.

4. Under each picture write the name of the item, a description of it, the color, size, and price of the item, and a catalog number. Use your own words to make each item sound desirable to a shopper.

5. Decide on a name for your catalog and design a cover.

6. Design an order form and include a place for the customer's name and address, the descriptive information for the items, and the totals.

VARIATIONS:

1. As a special project, have students use a story from their reading book or information from a social studies unit as a reference for designing a catalog that features items from a different time period (past or future).

2. Have students use a computer data base program to create sample order forms.

3. Have students simulate a TV home buying service. Tell them to choose items found in the classroom and set them up for display as if they were to be photographed for on-air viewing. Have students also write the dialogue for the voice-over announcer.

To Whom It May Concern

After selecting a product that they especially like or one that they think could be improved, students write a letter to the manufacturer to express their opinions.

Reading/Language Arts Skills: **writing—business letters • grammar and usage—sentences • handwriting • spelling • mechanics of writing—capitalization, punctuation**

Curricular Areas: **social studies • home economics**

Materials: **product package labels that contain the manufacturer's address • writing paper • envelopes • postage stamps**

Students will be excited about the responses they receive when you teach them about the "power of the pen."

PREPARATION: Ask students to bring a postage stamp and a product package label to class. Labels should be from products they especially enjoy or products that they feel could be improved. Tell them to be sure the product label they choose includes the manufacturer's address.

DIRECTIONS:

1. *(Prewriting:)* Today we will be writing to the manufacturers of the products you have selected. Before we begin, decide whether you will be writing a letter to compliment the manufacturer on the wonderful item the company has produced, or whether you would like to suggest ways of improving the product. Then, on a piece of scratch paper, jot down a list of reasons you enjoy the product or a few suggestions for improving it.

2. (Review the format for a business letter.) Locate the name and address of the manufacturer on the product label. Use this information to write the heading and greeting of your letter.

3. *(Drafting:)* Now write a first draft of your letter, making sure you express your ideas clearly in complete sentences. Be positive and specific in your praise or suggestions for improvement.

4. *(Revising and Proofreading:)* (Have students reread and revise their letters to present their message as clearly as possible. Peer editing can be very helpful at this stage. Tell students to be sure to check for correct spelling, capitalization, and punctuation.)

5. *(Final Copy:)* Copy the revised version of your letter. Write the closing and add your signature to the bottom of your letter. (Explain to students that it's a good idea to keep a copy of business correspondence for possible follow-up and future reference.)

6. Neatly address your envelope. Don't forget the stamp! (Students may mail their own letters, or you may collect the letters and mail them all at once.)

7. (Wait to see students' excitement when they receive answers to their letters! Many companies include free samples or coupons in their replies.)

VARIATIONS:

1. If a word processor is available, assign students to work in small groups to draft, revise, and produce a final copy of a letter to a manufacturer.

2. After reading a local newspaper editorial page, have students write letters to the editor expressing their opinions about current events.

3. Students may enjoy the opportunity to write letters to their legislators, senators, representatives, or even the President!

For a Code, Take Lemon Syrup!

Students investigate one way stores code their price tags. They practice decoding to find out what the price markup is and make up their own codes.

Reading/Language Arts Skills: **writing—codes • comprehension—codes, following directions**

Curricular Areas: **mathematics**

Materials: **Activity Sheet 2-5 • (optional: empty product packages with price tags)**

There's a lot of intrigue in coded price labels at the drugstore. The codes may not be as innocent as they seem.

DISCUSSION:

In addition to the price, what information may be on a price tag? (invoice date, quantity ordered, store's cost) Why is information coded on these tags? (It helps keep track of which items are selling quickly and which items have been on the shelf for a long time and therefore need to be rotated to the front of the shelf or possibly be sent back to the manufacturer.)

What is meant by "list price"? (the amount listed as the price of an item; normally, the amount the consumer pays for an item) What is meant by the "store's cost"? (the amount the store paid for an item) Why is the list price higher? (to cover the store's profit as well as its expenses for rent, utilities, insurance, maintenance, employee wages, and so on)

DIRECTIONS:

1. (On the chalkboard, write a ten-letter word or words where no letter is repeated. Under the letters write the digits 0 through 9.)

   Example: M A G I C S T O R E
   0 1 2 3 4 5 6 7 8 9

   Some stores use a letter code to show their cost for products before they mark them up. Suppose, for example, a bottle of aspirin has the code "ER" on it. Using the code on the chalkboard, what number does "E" stand for? (9) What number does "R" stand for? (8) What was the store's cost for the bottle of aspirin? ($.98)

2. Using letters in place of numbers, how would you code items that cost the store: $.36, $2.90, and $68.34? Decimal points are not coded. (IT, GEM, TRIC)

3. What was the store's cost for items that were coded G O R, I M A, and R S T M? Remember to put decimal points back in. ($2.78, $3.01, $85.60)

4. (Practice with other code words, such as CLOTHESPIN, CORN FLAKES, MODEL TRAIN, OLD WATCHES, PAINT BRUSH, ROCKETSHIP. Have students choose code words to work from.)

5. Pick a ten-letter code word or words where no letter is repeated. On a piece of paper, write five letter codes and five prices. Have a friend change the letters to prices and the prices to letters using your code word.

6. (Have students complete Activity Sheet 2-5.)

Answers:

1. $2.09	5. $2.86	9. $25.00
2. $1.78	6. $9.80	10. $29.50
3. $1.35	7. $2.19	
4. $0.43	8. $4.55	

For a Code, Take Lemon Syrup!

There is a letter code on the price tags in a local drugstore. The code is based on:

L E M O N S Y R U P

0 1 2 3 4 5 6 7 8 9

Letters on each price tag tell what the store paid for each item. (An item coded "MSL" cost the store $2.50.) For each product below, find the store's cost.

ITEM	LIST PRICE	CODE	STORE'S COST
1. Bandages	$ 2.29	MLP	_____
2. Vitamins	$ 2.45	ERU	_____
3. Shampoo	$ 2.98	EOS	_____
4. Dental Floss	$ 1.19	LNO	_____
5. Thermometer	$ 2.98	MUY	_____
6. Hair Dryer	$15.50	PUL	_____
7. Camera Film	$ 4.98	MEP	_____
8. Hot Water Bottle	$ 6.95	NSS	_____
9. Crutches	$35.00	MSLL	_____
10. Electric Crayons	$30.00	MPSL	_____

Dial M-Y P-H-O-N-E Number

Students use the letters and numbers on the telephone dial to make up personalized phone numbers for businesses and people.

Reading/Language Arts Skills: **writing—codes • comprehension—codes • creative expression • spelling**

Curricular Areas: **mathematics**

Materials: **Activity Sheet 2-6**

There's nothing phone-y about this activity! It's easy to dial—and easy to do!

DISCUSSION: What are the numbers and letters on the buttons on a telephone dial? Why do some commercials give a phone number and then repeat it as words? ("226-8742, that's 22 MUSIC" or "Need an exterminator? Call 837-6483, that's TERMITE") What would the phone number be for PEANUTS? (732-6887)

DIRECTIONS: (Have students complete Activity Sheet 2-6.)

Answers:

1. 496-6245
2. 336-8437
3. 847-3663
4. 278-2287
5. 654-6397
6. 247-7678
7. 928-3282
8. 767-7625
9. 269-5483
10. 742-6766
11. 342-6663
12. 726-2253

VARIATION: For more of a challenge, have children do this activity in reverse. Give all the digits in a phone number and ask students to find the word or words that the numbers stand for. Don't forget to give some clues. For example, phone numbers having to do with restaurants: 887-5397 (turkeys), 774-6224 (spinach), 683-3467 (muffins), 672-6437 (oranges).

Dial M-Y P-H-O-N-E Number

Some businesses have special phone numbers in which some or all of the numbers stand for letters that make up a word. Use the numbers and letters on this phone to figure out the phone numbers below.

PITTS-BURGERS

FAST FOOD TO GO

DIAL: BUR-GERS

Pitts-Burgers phone number is 287-4377!

A. What are the phone numbers of these businesses?

1. Hardware Store	496-NAIL	__ __ __ — __ __ __ __
2. Men's Clothing Store	336-TIES	__ __ __ — __ __ __ __
3. Sandwich Shop	847-FOOD	__ __ __ — __ __ __ __
4. Pet Shop	278-CATS	__ __ __ — __ __ __ __
5. TV Station	654-NEWS	__ __ __ — __ __ __ __
6. Pacific Airline	AIR-PORT	__ __ __ — __ __ __ __
7. Computer Company	928-DATA	__ __ __ — __ __ __ __
8. Pop Music Store	POP-ROCK	__ __ __ — __ __ __ __
9. Hobby Shop	269-KITE	__ __ __ — __ __ __ __
10. Beauty Shop	SHA-MPOO	__ __ __ — __ __ __ __
11. Jewelry Store	DIA-MOND	__ __ __ — __ __ __ __
12. Breakfast Shop	PAN-CAKE	__ __ __ — __ __ __ __

B. Make a word phone number for YOU! Base it on something special about yourself.

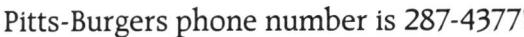

C. Make a word phone number for a friend.

__ __ __ — __ __ __ __.

D. Make word phone numbers for some businesses in your town.

A Classy Phone Book

Students create a class telephone directory. They use alphabetizing, guide letters, organizational skills, and their creative talents in this activity.

Reading/Language Arts Skills: **study skills—alphabetical order, telephone book • handwriting**

Curricular Areas: **mathematics • art**

Materials: **class roster • writing paper • colored paper • stapler, brads, or yarn • (optional: yellow page—page 113)**

This "class-y" activity calls on your students' creativity and handwriting skills.

PREPARATION: Prepare a class roster; the names should *not* be in alphabetical order.

DISCUSSION: What kinds of information are found in a telephone book? How is this information arranged? (in alphabetical order by last name)

DIRECTIONS:
1. (*Alphabetizing:*) (Distribute a class list or have students write their names in random order on the chalkboard.) Please put this list of students' names in alphabetical order by last name.

2. (*Collecting Information:*) Now we are ready to add addresses and phone numbers. If someone does not have a phone number, we'll write "unlisted." (One by one, have students write their addresses and phone numbers on the chalkboard for others to copy, or have them recite the information while class members write it down.)

3. (*Arranging Information:*) Now you will decide how to arrange this information in your phone book, how to organize the information on each page, how much to put on each page, and so on.

   (Give each student some writing paper.) Carefully plan how many names will fit on each page. Include guide letters and page numbers at the top of each page.

4. (*Adding More Information:*) What other phone numbers should your phone book include? (emergency phone numbers; frequently called numbers; extension numbers of school staff members, such as the principal, secretary, nurse, custodian; and

so on) Add them to the front or back pages of your book. (Students may also design yellow pages to add to their phone books or use the one on page 113.)

5. (*Creative Design:*) You will complete your phone book by putting it together inside a cover and fastening it with staples, brads, or yarn. Design your own cover. (The front cover could include the class name, teacher's name, room number, and the date it was completed. The back might include a school or neighborhood map, local ZIP codes, a design for the 911 emergency number, or advertising.)

VARIATION: If a computer is available, students may use a data base program to record, arrange, and print their telephone books.

Name That Word!

Players move around a game board, landing on spaces marked with the letters of the alphabet, and name words associated with a given consumer topic. After learning the basic game, students compose consumer cards to add excitement.

Reading/Language Arts Skills:	**writing—descriptive paragraphs • vocabulary—content area words • comprehension—classifying**
Curricular Areas:	**art • home economics • social studies • science**
Materials:	**game board (page 277) • game spinner (page 276) • paper clip and pencil • playing piece for each student (a coin, button, or ring) • index cards • (optional: old magazines and catalogs, paste, scissors)**

Words, words, words—so many ways to name and describe consumer items!

PREPARATION:

To make spinner:

1. Duplicate a game spinner (page 276) for each group of two to four players.

2. Fill in the five sections with 1, 2, 3, 4, 5.

To make game board:

1. Duplicate a game board (page 277) for each group of players.

2. (Optional: To make large game boards, make an overhead transparency of the game board (page 277) and trace around a projected image on tagboard or stiffening fabric used for interfacing.)

To make consumer cards:

(Note: This game can be played with or without these cards. In any case, it's a good idea for students to play *without* the cards first. This way, students will become familiar with the game—and it will start them thinking about "situation" ideas for the cards.)

1. Students will work in groups. Each group should decide on a consumer topic for their game, such as food, clothing, animals, jobs, and so on. Then the group should brainstorm ideas for different situations. One person should take notes. (See VARIATIONS for suggestions for other consumer topics.)

2. Each group must come up with a set of six or more cards that describe a consumer situation and that ask players to name one or more items.

EXAMPLES: "You live at the North Pole. Name something you might wear that begins with this letter of the alphabet."

"Your cousin Hattie collects (and wears) unusual hats. You want to make her one for a gift. Name two things, beginning with this letter, that you'll use to decorate her hat."

DIRECTIONS: To complete game boards:

1. Have students fill in each of the 26 spaces on their game boards with a different letter of the alphabet. They can be written in order (*A* in the first space, *B* in the next, and so on) or they can be mixed up (*F, Y, N, B,* . . .).

2. (Optional: To make a game board for a specific consumer topic, such as a "Food" game board:) Have students cut out pictures related to their consumer topics (apples, bread, cheese, and so on) from old magazines and catalogs and paste them around the border of their game boards.

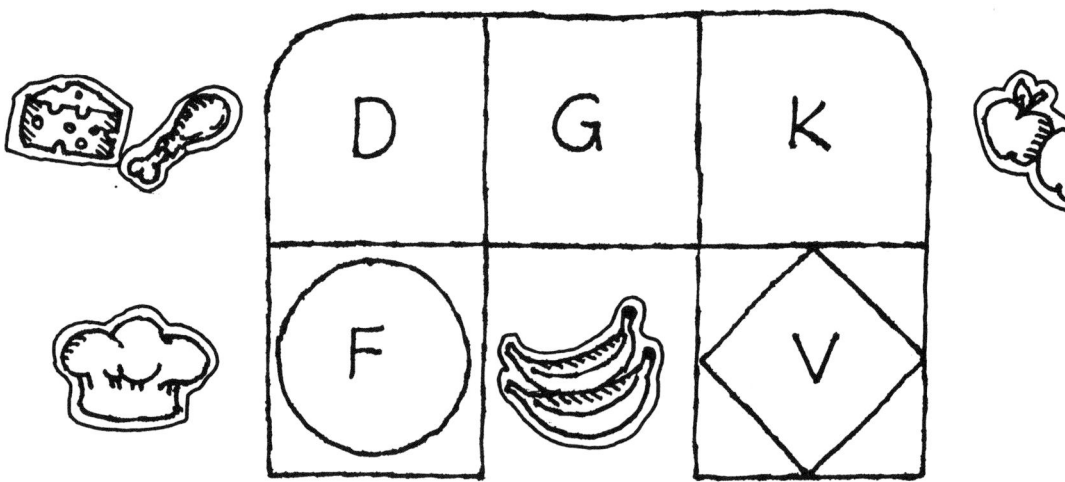

To play "Name That Word!":

1. Tell students to keep in mind the consumer topic their group has chosen.

2. Players spin—the player who spins the highest number goes first. This person spins again and moves his or her piece the given number of spaces.

3. In order to stay on that space, the player must name a word that starts with the letter on the space and is associated with the group's consumer topic. Otherwise the player must move back one space and name a word for that letter.

Chapter 2: Writing

4. If consumer cards are being used, every time a player spins a "5" he or she must take a card and follow the directions on the card. If the player is unable to follow the directions, he or she loses a turn.

5. The winner is the first person to reach the finish line.

VARIATIONS:

A. ADVERTISING GAME

Name a word that might be used in an advertisement for a product from a certain kind of store.

Pet Store: animals, bunny, cuddly, . . .
Restaurant: . . . delicious, eggs, fresh, . . .
Fabric Shop: . . . ribbon, silk, thread, . . .

B. BUYING GAME

Name some things you can buy.

To wear: apron, boots, coat, . . .
To eat: . . . melon, nuts, oatmeal, . . .
To play with: . . . xylophone, yoyo, zither.

C. CONSERVING GAME

Name something we want to recycle rather than throw away: aluminum, bottles, cans, . . .
Something we want to conserve: . . . energy, fuel, gas, . . .
Something to be saved: . . . newspapers, old coins, photographs, . . .

D. DRIVING GAME

Name something that provides some sort of transportation: automobile, boat, carriage, . . . yacht, zebra.

E. EARNING GAME

Name a way to earn money: acting, baking, caring for children, . . . zipper repairing. (Nouns can be emphasized by naming a career: architect, builder, chef, . . . yodeler, zookeeper.)

F. FOOD GAME

Name a food item: apple, bread, cheese, . . . zucchini.

G. GAMES, GAMES, . . . AND MORE GAMES

Gardening, hobbies, investments, jobs, . . . and a multitude of consumer topics to provide vocabulary practice all year.

Walk Softly and Carry a Sharp Pencil

Students take a walk in the school neighborhood and note the path they are following. When they return to the classroom, they write directions for the route they followed.

Reading/Language Art Skills: **writing—directions • spelling • speaking—giving directions • study skills—taking notes (optional: maps)**

Curricular Areas: **mathematics • physical education • social studies**

Materials: **paper and pencils • clipboards, books, or other sturdy objects for students to write on while walking**

Don't save this activity for a rainy day! Save it for a clear day when you and your students are restless and feel an urge to get out of the classroom.

PREPARATION:
1. Decide on a destination for a walk with your class (such as a nearby park, the post office, or the library).
2. Make sure each student has paper, a pencil, and something sturdy to write on.

DISCUSSION:
What are some occupations where workers are frequently asked to give directions around town? (gas station attendant, bus driver, police officer, mail carrier) What are some ways of making directions clear and easy to follow? (Describe landmarks; indicate intersections, stop signs or traffic lights; count blocks; name streets; indicate left and right turns; and so on.)

DIRECTIONS:
1. As we walk to the park (post office, library), please take careful notes on how we get there. Include landmarks, the number of streets we cross, and other important information in your notes.
2. Now and then, we'll stop for a few minutes so that you can write. Note the directions we turn, right or left (north, south, east, or west).
3. (Once you have reached your destination:) As we walk back to school, double-check your notes. Carefully count the streets we cross again. What will be different on the way back? (Directions will be in reverse order; left turns change to right, and so on.)

4. (Back in the classroom:) Please use your notes to write clear directions for walking from the school to the park (post office, library).

5. (After students have written directions:) Let's have volunteers read their directions to the class. (Have volunteers come to the front of the room and read their directions.) Were the directions clear? Were important landmarks and intersections described carefully? Were streets named? Were left and right turns indicated?

VARIATIONS:

1. Students may enjoy drawing a map to show the route taken on the walk.

2. Have students give oral directions on how to get to their homes from school.

3. If your school has the equipment, have students make a video of the walk.

Quick and Easy

A. SHOPPING LIST

1. On a piece of paper, make a shopping list of all the ingredients needed to make a delicious stew or soup (tasty tacos, mouth-watering pizza, nutritious breakfast, colossal salad, or another favorite food).

2. (Have students rewrite their lists, this time grouping items by where they would be found in the supermarket—produce section, dairy case, frozen food section, and so on.)

B. FOOD FOR THOUGHT

1. What are your favorite foods? Let's choose one and brainstorm adjectives to describe it. (List the adjectives on the chalkboard.)

2. (From the list, have students create an adjective poem in which the first line names the food and each subsequent line consists of one adjective. Students can also write the adjectives in the shape of the item.)

Pizza

Hot,
Crusty,
Spicy,
Cheesy,
Easy,
Good!

3. (On another day have students create an adjective poem that focuses on a different category, such as a favorite sport, a hobby, a movie, or a famous person.)

C. A CHALKBOARD COLLAGE OF FEELINGS

(This Quick and Easy idea is also meaningful—especially if students have already done Activity 3-5, "Tune In to Feelings." For another idea using used greeting cards, see Quick and Easy Activity 7-7J, "Crazy Mixed-Up Greetings," page 202.)

1. (As you read a commercial greeting card to the class, have students think about the feelings they experience from the message. Then have students, one at a time, write those feelings on the chalkboard until it is filled with feelings.)

2. (If there are enough used cards, let each student independently read one, consider his or her feelings, and write them on the chalkboard. This allows students to be more aware of their own feelings and be less affected by someone else's reading.)

D. STORY STRETCH

1. (Write a one-sentence story starter related to consumerism on the chalkboard. For example: "One Saturday, Molly decided to earn money by starting a dog-bathing business," or "The TV commercial said it would get any stain out, but Bruce knew better.")

2. (Call on a student.) Please read the story starter, and then add a sentence to it. When you are finished, choose another classmate to continue the story.

3. (The story may be continued as time allows. The last student should add a sentence that ends the story.)

4. (Variation: Have each student write a one-sentence story starter on a piece of paper and then pass it to another student, who adds a sentence and passes it on. After the last person ends the story, collect all the "stretched-out" stories and read them to the class or post them on a bulletin board.)

E. COMPOSE YOURSELF

1. Imagine you are running for class (club or committee) president. Compose a 25-word description of yourself that could be printed in the school newspaper or in an election pamphlet.

2. (On another day, students can "compose" themselves in a letter format to be sent to a new pen pal or a potential employer.)

3. (See Quick and Easy Activity 3-9I, "Introducing . . . You," page 94, for a quick listening and speaking activity to do another day.)

F. BRAND NAME WORDS

1. (Write the name of a cereal or other product on the chalkboard—for example, *Apple Crackles*. Have students make as many words as possible from the letters: *ape, cape, scrape, pack, lack, please, apparel,* and so on.)

2. (Repeat the activity using the name of a popular store, car model, magazine, or type of sports equipment.)

G. SUPERMARKET ANAGRAMS

1. (Write some or all of the words listed below on the chalkboard.)

2. Try to rearrange the letters in each word to make another word.

TUNA	(aunt)
MEAT	(mate, team)
BREAD	(beard)
SALT	(last)
PANS	(snap, naps, span)
PIE TIN	(tie pin)
SIGN	(sing)
PEACH	(cheap)

3. Think of another supermarket anagram and give it to a classmate to solve. (Explain to the class that an anagram is a word or phrase in which all the letters can be rearranged to form another word or phrase.)

H. LOST AND FOUND

1. Write a Lost and Found notice for the sweater you lost over the weekend. Include a description of your sweater, where and when it was lost, your name, and an address or phone number where you can be reached. Use abbreviations to save space.

2. (Have students repeat the activity for other lost articles: a pet, watch, bicycle, wallet, and so on.)

3. (Give each group of students a similar looking item, such as a tennis shoe, a ball point pen, or an apple. Allow each group ten minutes to write a list, as long as possible, of

details describing the "unique" qualities of their item. Then put the items in a pile and have a student from each group identify the group's item. The student must justify why the item belongs to his or her group by referring to the group's list of details.)

I. THE MAIL MUST GO THROUGH

(Optional Preparation: Set up a real mailbox or construct one from a shoebox. If you like, staple it to a bulletin board.)

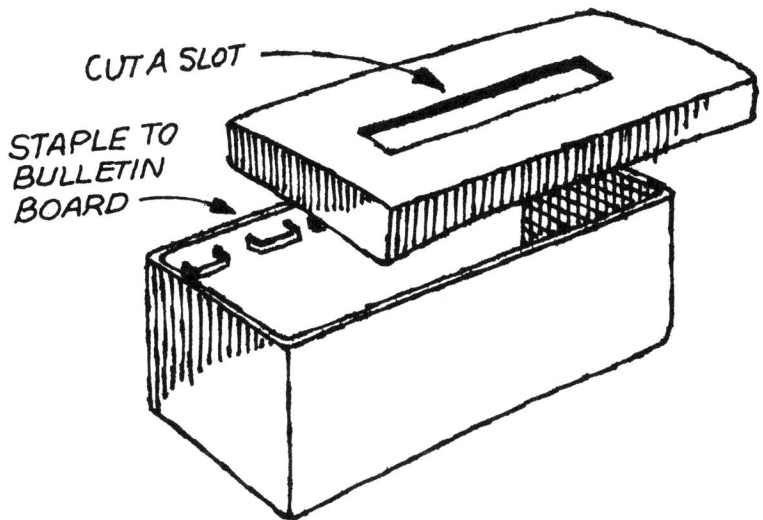

1. (Optional: Make copies of the telegrams on pages 211–212 or the greeting cards on pages 184–186 for students to use.) During the ten minutes we have before lunch, write a note, telegram, letter, or card, and put it in the mailbox for a classmate. (Students may enjoy writing letters to a classmate who's having a birthday, is new to the class, has been sick, is moving, and so on.) Our class mail carrier will distribute the mail after lunch.

2. (On another day, pair up students and have them write quick letters to each other.)

3. (For an even quicker activity, see Quick and Easy Activity 7-7H, "Thanks," on page 201.)

Listening and Speaking

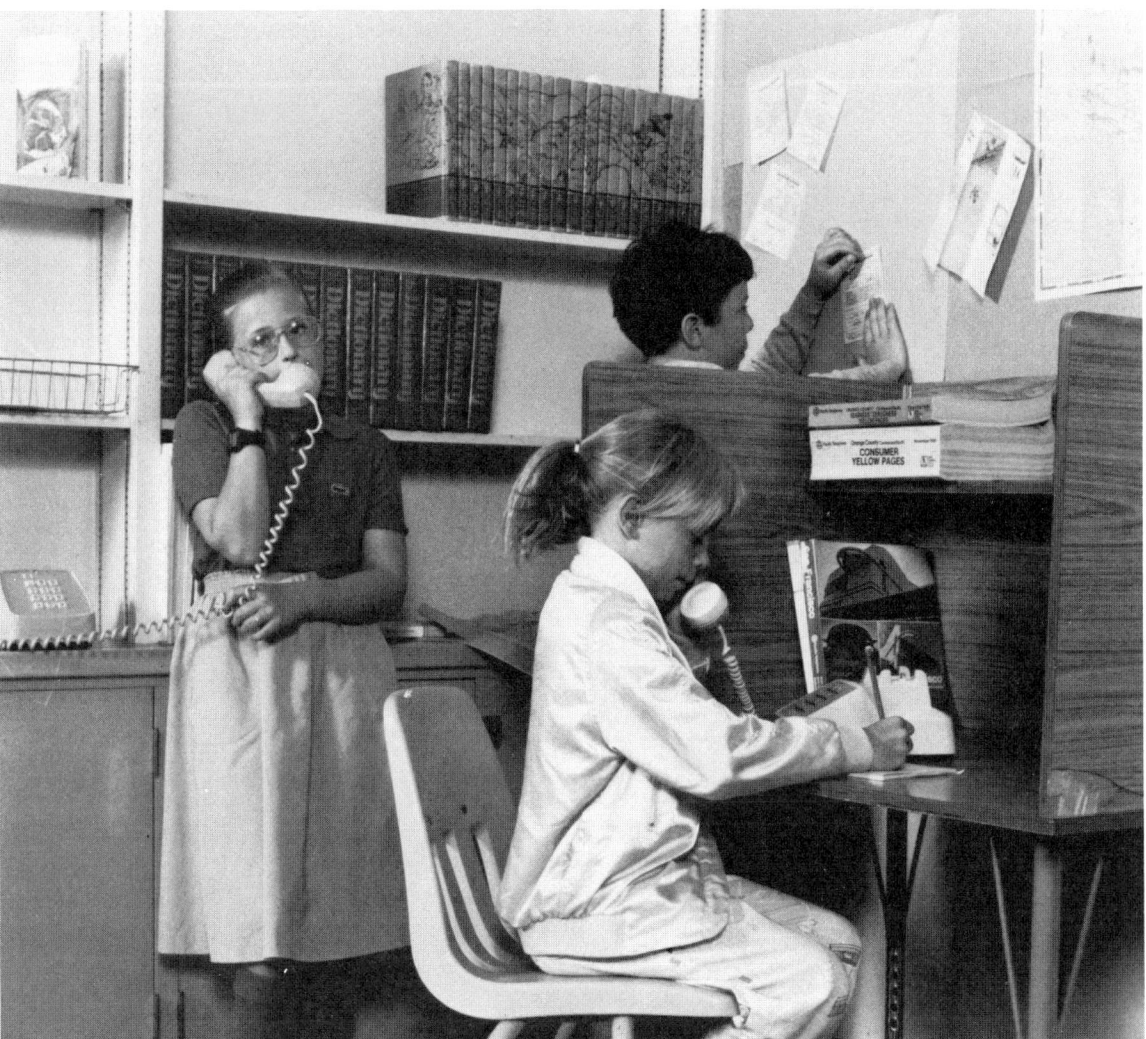

Take a Message, Please   Activity 3-1

1. *Take a Message, Please*
2. *A Picture Is Worth a Thousand Words!*
3. *Go with the Flow Chart*
4. *Buyer Beware!*
5. *Tune In to Feelings*
6. *Meaningful Music*
7. *Taste and Tell*
8. *The Energy User Game*

9. *Quick and Easy*
   A. *I Scream for Ice Cream*
   B. *A Word from Our Sponsor*
   C. *Consumer Charades*
   D. *Phone Fun-damentals*
   E. *Speak Out!*
   F. *What You "Auto" Know About Insurance*
   G. *Commercials and Jazzy Jingles*
   H. *Name That Slogan!*
   I. *Introducing You!*

73

Communication—it is one of the most important life skills to learn! When students become good listeners and effective speakers, they do better in school. And communication skills are essential for students as consumers to protect their own rights, experience consumer confidence, and make better decisions about spending and saving money.

The activities in this chapter will help students develop these important consumer skills. "Take a Message, Please" and "Phone Fun-damentals" give students an opportunity to develop confidence using the telephone. Participating in a taste test ("Taste and Tell") and listening to records and tapes ("Tune In to Feelings") help students learn what influences their buying. They also have the opportunity to express their feelings when consumer problems arise ("Speak Out!").

As students get involved in these activities, they'll begin to think of ways to communicate more effectively in their own lives. Encourage them to write letters, make phone calls, or use some other means to get in touch with relatives or friends.

Learning, feeling good, and making others feel good—a great combination for any class!

So . . . don't hang up! Just dial "Information" in this chapter. You're bound to get a busy signal—a signal that means your students are communicating and learning!

Take a Message, Please

Students practice giving and taking telephone messages to become more effective users of this universal and essential utility. *(See photo, page 73.)*

Reading/Language Arts Skills: listening—listening for information • speaking—giving information • writing—messages • spelling • drama—role playing

Curricular Areas: social studies

Materials: telephone message forms (page 77)

This activity is sure to "ring the bell" with your kids and provide high-interest learning!

PREPARATION: Duplicate enough copies of the telephone message forms (page 77) so that each student will have several.

DISCUSSION: Why do we use the telephone? (to talk to friends, to give and receive messages, to find out information, and so on) Have you ever taken a message and had trouble writing it down? (Have students share individual experiences.) What information is important to get when taking a message? (the caller's name and telephone number)

DIRECTIONS: Find a friend to be your telephone partner. One of you will pretend to call the other on the telephone. Using the following telephone conversation ideas, take turns being the caller and the person answering. Read the message back each time to be sure you've written it correctly.

1. The manager of the Main Street Bank calls and leaves a message with you for your parents. One of their checks has bounced, and they are to call back as soon as possible! Write the message on the message form as the bank manager (your partner) gives you the information.

2. You forgot to bring your spelling list home to study. Call your friend and ask him or her to read the list as you write the words down. Use your class spelling words for this activity.

3. Call and invite your friend to a special party you are having. Give the date, starting and ending time, place, and kind of party. Your friend will write the information on the message form.

4. You want to find the best price in town for pizza. Call several pizza restaurants and ask the price for a particular size and kind of pizza. Write the information down for each pizza parlor.

5. You need a haircut. Call a barber or beauty shop and make an appointment. Write the date and time of the appointment on the message form.

VARIATIONS:

1. Have students choose one of the above situations and speak very quickly. Students will need to ask their partners to slow down or repeat information in order to take the message correctly.

2. Have students use a word processor to develop specialized telephone message forms for themselves or for different businesses or organizations.

Telephone Message Forms
(Use for Activities 3-1, 4-4)

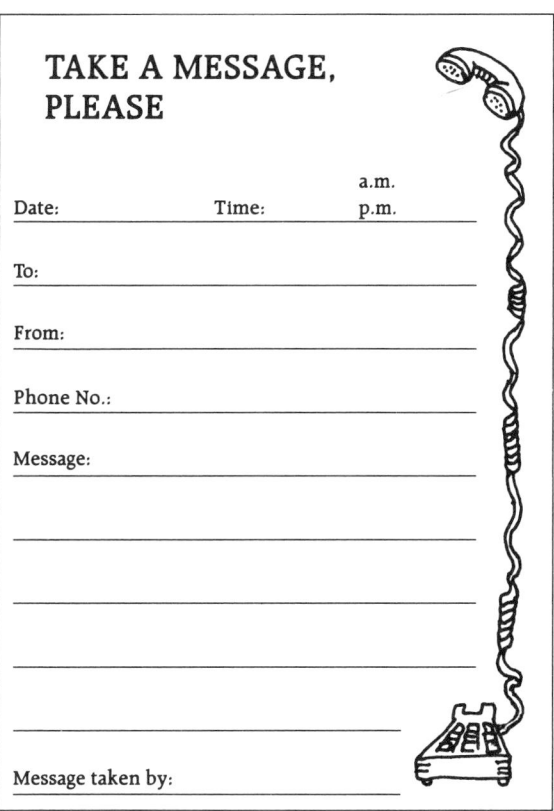

TAKE A MESSAGE, PLEASE

Date: _____ Time: _____ a.m. _____ p.m.

To: _____

From: _____

Phone No.: _____

Message: _____

_____

_____

_____

_____

Message taken by: _____

TAKE A MESSAGE, PLEASE

Date: _____ Time: _____ a.m. _____ p.m.

To: _____

From: _____

Phone No.: _____

Message: _____

_____

_____

_____

_____

Message taken by: _____

TAKE A MESSAGE, PLEASE

Date: _____ Time: _____ a.m. _____ p.m.

To: _____

From: _____

Phone No.: _____

Message: _____

_____

_____

_____

_____

Message taken by: _____

TAKE A MESSAGE, PLEASE

Date: _____ Time: _____ a.m. _____ p.m.

To: _____

From: _____

Phone No.: _____

Message: _____

_____

_____

_____

_____

Message taken by: _____

A Picture Is Worth a Thousand Words!

Students make collages to illustrate different ways that nonverbal communication takes place.

Reading/Language Arts Skills: nonverbal communication—body language, mime

Curricular Areas: art • mathematics • social studies

Materials: one or more of the following: magazines, newspapers, addressed pieces of mail (such as envelopes, brochures, and catalogs) • paper • scissors • paste or tape

---

Have you ever thought about all the ways we communicate? This activity may produce some unique and unexpected responses.

DISCUSSION: What are some ways that we communicate with people without using words? (numbers, pictures, symbols, facial expressions, body language) Give some examples of how numbers are used to communicate. (ZIP code, street number, apartment number, date, permit number, area code, phone number, page number, catalog number) Give some examples of how pictures, symbols, and body language are used to communicate. (logos identify businesses or products; arrows and pictographs show direction, direct traffic, and inform; handshakes show friendliness) In what ways can music communicate? (soft music may set a serious or romantic mood, bugle taps signal the end of day, and so on)

DIRECTIONS: (Students may work alone or in small groups. Provide materials for each group or individual.)

1. We're going to make collages to illustrate the many ways that we communicate. Look through the materials for numbers, pictures of facial expressions and gestures, logos, symbols, and so on.

2. Cut out any examples of communication you find. Arrange the items on paper and paste or tape them in place. You may want to group your items in categories (numbers, body language, symbols, and so on) and label each with its category.

3. When you are finished, share your collage with the class.

VARIATION: Students, in small groups, can mime examples of nonverbal messages. For example, they can demonstrate body language that shows different emotions (happiness, surprise, boredom, impatience, and so on).

Go with the Flow Chart!

Students practice making flow charts for events in given consumer situations; then they create their own flow charts.

Reading/Language Arts Skills: **comprehension—sequence of events • writing—directions • study skills—flow charts**

Curricular Areas: **social studies**

Materials: **Activity Sheet 3-3 • scissors • paper**

Computer programs (called SOFTware) tell computers (the HARDware) what to do. So—since the whole idea of computers can be HARD for students to understand—here's a SOFT way to explain it.

DISCUSSION: What is a flow chart? (a diagram that shows the steps to complete a task) How do computers know what to do? (Computer programmers break tasks into steps, then diagram the steps using a flow chart. Flow-charting is the basic concept behind the programs that give instructions to computers.)

DIRECTIONS:

1. Please take a piece of paper and cut it into four equal pieces.

2. Think of four steps you take when dialing a phone (addressing an envelope, buying something from a vending machine, and so on). Write each step on a piece of paper.

3. Now mix up the steps and exchange your pieces with a friend. Put the pieces in a logical sequence, then check each other's work.

4. (Have students complete Activity Sheet 3-3. You may want to take the time to explain the symbols and do the first flow chart as a class activity.)

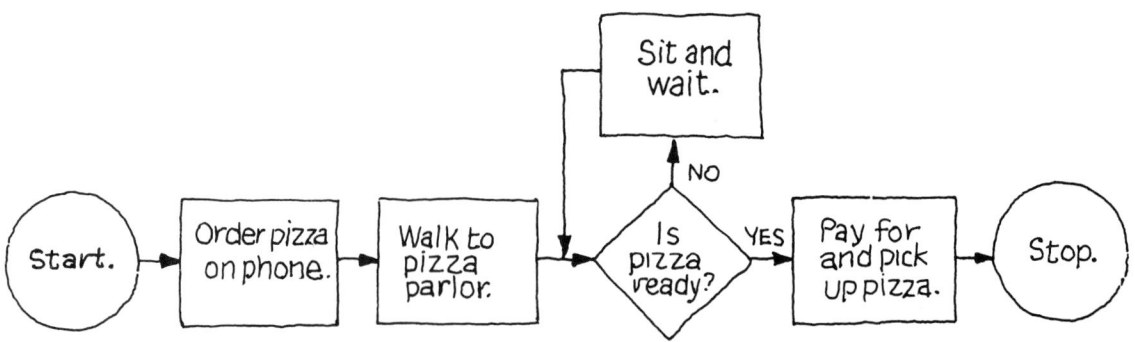

Go with the Flow Chart!

A flow chart uses different shapes to represent steps in a task.

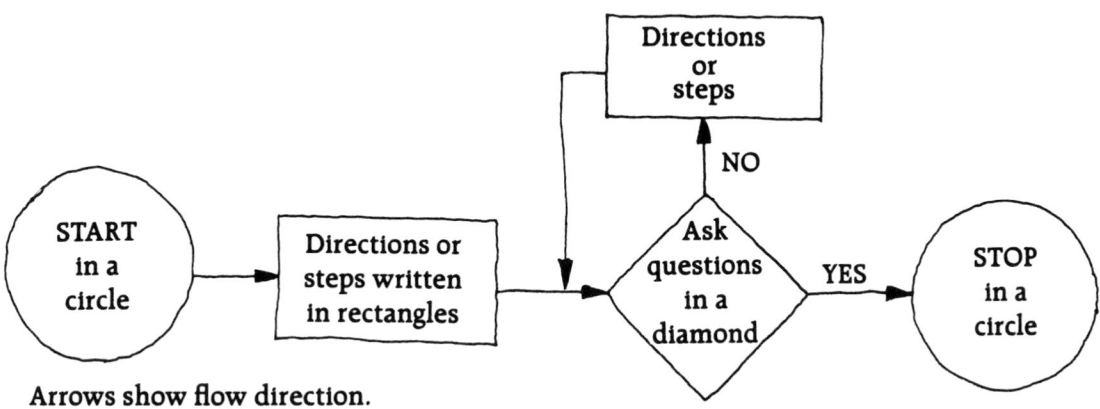

Arrows show flow direction.

1. Fill in the flow chart below with the following steps for ordering a pizza:

   Start. Order pizza on phone. Walk to pizza parlor. Is pizza ready? Sit and wait. Pay for and pick up pizza. Stop.

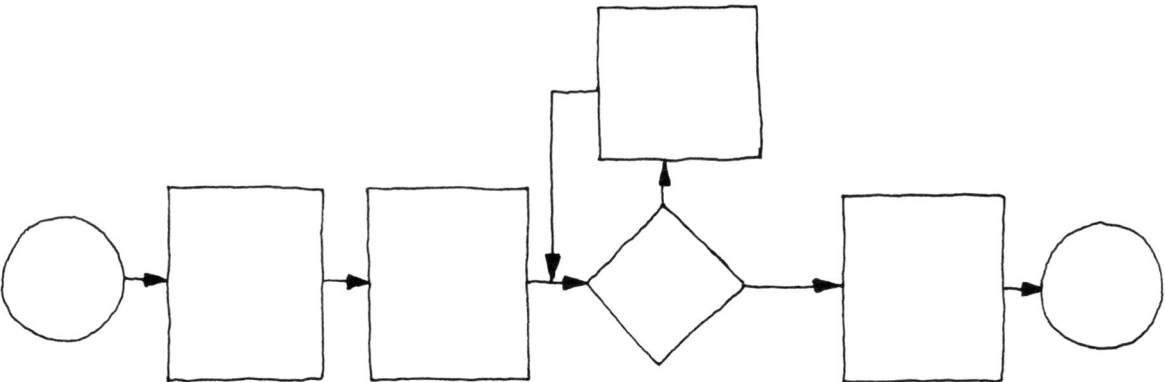

2. List, in order, the steps involved in buying a pet monkey. On the back of this paper, make a flow chart to show the steps.

   _____

   _____

   _____

   _____

   _____

3. For more practice, try flow-charting some of the following:
   - sending party invitations
   - ordering something from a catalog
   - booting a computer disk
   - making a sandwich
   - buying a new bike
   - subscribing to a magazine

Buyer Beware!

Students role play bait-and-switch advertising techniques and then compare the advertised price of an item with the prices of other brands.

Reading/Language Arts Skills: **listening—critical listening • critical thinking—analyzing bait-and-switch advertisements • drama—role playing**

Curricular Areas: **social studies • mathematics**

A bit of drama in class will provide a delightful change of pace and an opportunity for students to display their finest high-pressure sales tactics!

DISCUSSION: In what ways are salespersons helpful to buyers? In what ways are they sometimes not so helpful? What are some of the high-pressure techniques that salespersons sometimes use? Why do they use these tactics?

DIRECTIONS:

1. We're going to analyze a high-pressure sales tactic known as "bait and switch." In this sales technique, you see an ad or a window display for a low-priced item: "Roller skates at rock-bottom prices!" This is the "bait" to get you inside the store. Once you're inside, the salesperson tries to make you "switch" to a higher priced pair of roller skates.

2. Pretend that you see an ad for a 10-speed bike for $99.00 and decide to buy it. When you go into the store, the salesperson says, "Well, this bike isn't really *that* good. But, I've got this other bike that's only $159.95 and it will hold up longer because . . . ."

3. Would two of you please act out this example? Now, act it out again, but this time make the buyer more assertive, so that the salesperson really has to work. (After they've acted out the example, ask students to discuss the bait-and-switch tactic. You may also want to have them calculate the price difference between the two bikes.)

4. Now work in groups of two or three to make up some more bait-and-switch examples. Use different types of stores and merchandise. Take a few minutes to plan and practice. (Encourage students to discuss each situation.)

5. (Optional: Choose some of the role-playing situations and calculate the difference in the prices of the items.)

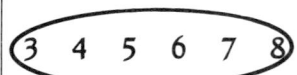
Tune In to Feelings

Students listen to a recorded radio or television commercial and try to identify the feelings they are experiencing; then they discuss how the commercial affects consumer feelings and buying attitudes.

Reading/Language Arts Skills: **listening—critical listening • critical thinking—expressing opinions, analyzing cause and effect • writing—descriptive phrases**

Curricular Areas: **social studies**

Materials: **tape recorder and blank cassette tape**

As a learning station or group activity, students will be eager to "tune in" and discover what is "turning on" their feelings!

PREPARATION: Record on a cassette tape two different radio or television commercials geared to the interests of your students.

DISCUSSION: Why would a company want a commercial to affect your feelings as you listen to it? (to create a desire to buy the product) What are some feelings that you might experience when listening to a commercial? (excitement, pleasure, hunger, thirst, envy, and so on)

DIRECTIONS:
1. Listen carefully and quietly to the commercial. As you listen, try to identify what feelings you are experiencing.

2. When the commercial has ended, take a few moments to write down your feelings on a piece of paper. This is a quiet, thoughtful activity, so please don't discuss it right now with your friends.

3. When you are ready, quietly go to the chalkboard and write some words that describe your feelings. (Variation: You can record student responses on the chalkboard or on chart paper.)

4. (After the chalkboard is filled with words, continue with a discussion.) What feelings did many of you experience that were the same? What elements of the commercial caused you to feel that way? (music, catchy words, popular personality, and so on) Would you buy the product? Why or why not?

VARIATIONS:
1. At a learning station, have students listen to recorded commercials and then write about their feelings and the aspects of the commercial they think caused those feelings.

2. Do Quick and Easy activities 3-9G, "Commercials and Jazzy Jingles," page 93, and 2-10C, "A Chalkboard Collage of Feelings," page 69.

Meaningful Music

Students listen to the words and music of a popular song and consider how it makes them feel. They decide what it is about the lyrics that might affect their decision to purchase a recording of the song.

Reading/Language Arts Skills: **listening—critical listening • writing—song lyrics • creative expression • critical thinking—expressing opinions**

Curricular Areas: **music • social studies**

Materials: **tape recorder • tape recording of a popular song • copy of lyrics • (optional: song on page 280 • VCR and television)**

Young people buy more records than any other group of people. This activity asks them to take a critical look at what they're buying.

PREPARATION: Make, purchase, or borrow a tape recording of a popular song. Duplicate copies of the words to the song for each student. Your local library, a music store, or your students can help you select the song and locate a copy of its lyrics.

DISCUSSION: What are some ways that music affects people? (relaxes, energizes, and so on) How do the lyrics influence people? (suggest new ideas, reinforce feelings, entertain, and so on) Do you listen carefully to song lyrics?

DIRECTIONS:
1. (Play the song for the class.) Let's listen to this song together.
2. (Give each student a copy of the song lyrics.) As you listen to the song again, please follow along by reading the lyrics.
3. (After hearing the song a second time:) Read the lyrics and think about how the words make you feel. Did you feel differently when you knew all the words? (Have students share their feelings with the rest of the class.)
4. (Optional:) Are there any words or phrases you think should be changed? Mark the changes. If you like the lyrics as they are, don't make any changes. (Have students share their ideas with the class and explain why they did or did not make changes. Ask students if they would buy the tape or album as is or with the changes.)

VARIATION: If you have access to a VCR, record a television commercial in which music is played. Have students note how the music influences their attitudes toward the product. Ask questions such as, "How do the lyrics and music affect your desire to buy the product?" "What feelings do you experience when listening to the lyrics and music?"

Taste and Tell

Working in small groups, students taste three brands of the same food product and choose one to promote on a TV commercial.

Reading/Language Arts Skills: listening—critical listening • critical thinking—comparing and contrasting, evaluating advertisements, expressing opinions • writing—descriptive phrases • creative expression • grammar and usage—adjectives • drama

Curricular Areas: home economics • mathematics • music • art

Materials: **Activity Sheet 3-7 • three different brands of the same food item, enough for each student to have a small taste (such as canned fruit or vegetables, cereal, peanuts, crackers) • napkins, small paper plates, plastic spoons • drawing paper • crayons or markers**

Students will sink their teeth into this activity and digest some important practice in listening and speaking skills!

PREPARATION: Remove or cover the labels on each food container and relabel them *X, Y,* and *Z.*

DISCUSSION: Why do you think people choose certain brands of food? What are some factors that influence those choices? (packaging or labeling, commercial promises, catchy songs or jingles, price, taste, appearance, and so on)

DIRECTIONS:
1. (Divide the class into small groups. Pass out Activity Sheet 3-7 and samples of the three brands of the food item.)

2. (Have students taste the three different brands and then complete Activity Sheet 3-7.)

3. Now we're going to create some advertising for your favorite products. Think of a new brand name for the food item your group liked best. Design a new label or package for this product. Focus your advertising on the qualities that made it the best.

4. Discuss ways to advertise your product on television (such as drama, song, jingle, fantasy, use of a child star, association with a famous person).

5. Plan a TV commercial for your product. Assign parts to group members, practice it, and then perform it for the class.

6. (Optional: After each group performs, ask students to vote for the product they would buy and explain how the packaging and commercial affected that choice. Ask how taste affected their choice. Have them discuss which has a stronger impact on consumer choice, taste or advertising.)

Taste and Tell

Taste each brand of the food item. Then use the chart below to rate each brand. Use the following rating system.

1 = Very poor
2 = Poor
3 = Okay
4 = Good
5 = Very good

	BRAND X	BRAND Y	BRAND Z
FLAVOR			
SMELL			
APPEARANCE			
FRESHNESS			
Total			

In your group, add together the total scores for each brand.

Which brand received the highest overall score? _____

Make a list of adjectives or phrases that describe the good

qualities of the winning brand. _____

_____

_____

_____

_____

_____

_____

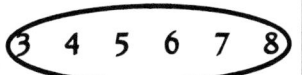

The Energy User Game

After students brainstorm a list of energy-using items, they play a guessing game about them.

Reading/Language Arts Skills: listening—critical listening • critical thinking—comparing and contrasting, classifying

Curricular Areas: science • home economics • social studies

Materials: index cards or small pieces of paper • paper bag

This game is sure to "energize" your students into being wise users and consumers of our valuable resources!

DISCUSSION: What is energy? (a source of power to make things work) What are some examples of energy sources? (electricity, gasoline, the sun, nuclear power, falling water, the wind, people's hands and feet) What are some products that use energy that we must pay for? (toasters, televisions, computers, lights, cars, electric trains, and so on) What are some things that do not cost money to power? (windmills, hand-cranked meat grinders, bicycles, wind-up toys, push lawn mowers, manual typewriters, and so on)

PREPARATION: 1. Class activity: On the chalkboard, make two column headings entitled *Money* and *No Money*. Ask students to think of energy-using products that cost money to run. List their responses under the *Money* heading on the chalkboard. Then, for each item in the *Money* column, ask students to name something that serves the same purpose but doesn't cost money to run. List their responses in the *No Money* column.

2. You or volunteers write each pair of items on a card, noting which item costs money to run and which doesn't. Mix up the cards in a paper bag. To play the guessing game, students will need at least 20 pairs of items. Suggestions:

vacuum cleaner	copy machine
broom	carbon paper
escalator	curling iron
stairs	curlers
calculator	electric typewriter
abacus	manual typewriter
gas heater	electric lamp
fireplace	candle

electric shaver	motorboat
razor	sailboat
food processor	electric clothes dryer
knife	clothesline
motorcycle	electric fan
bicycle	hand fan
electric mixer	word processor
hand mixer	pencil
stereo	chain saw
musical instrument	ax
electric blanket	sewing machine
comforter	needle and thread

3. Optional: As a homework assignment, have students think of more pairs of items.

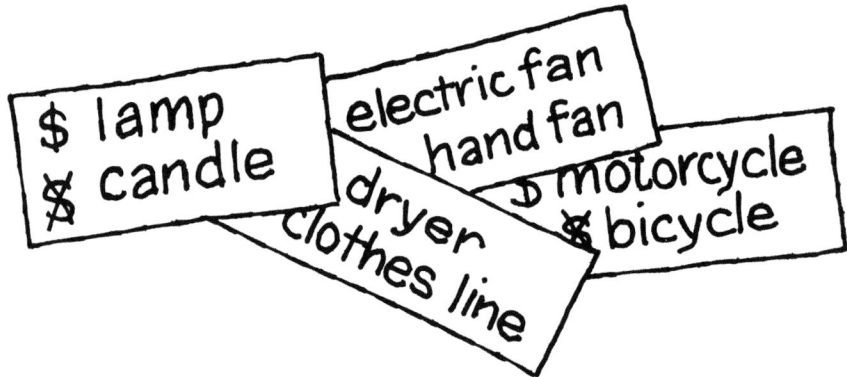

DIRECTIONS:

1. We're going to play a version of Twenty Questions. One person will pick a card with two energy-using items on it. One item costs money to run; the other doesn't. Then you will ask questions about the items that can be answered yes or no.

2. (Choose a student to come up and draw a card from the bag.) Look at the two energy-using items. Now class, you may ask questions about the items that can be answered yes or no. (Is the "money" energy user an electrical appliance? Do you use it in the kitchen? Is the "no money" energy user powered by hand?)

3. (Students take turns guessing until the two items have been named. The person who guessed correctly draws the next card.)

Quick and Easy

A. I SCREAM FOR ICE CREAM

1. Pretend you are at the supermarket and you see some ice cream you want your mother or father to buy. How will you convince her or him to buy it? (Would you scream? Cry? Beg? Give good reasons for buying it?) What reasons could you give?

2. Who would like to come to the front of the room and show us how you would persuade your mom or dad to buy the ice cream?

3. (On another day, focus on the other side.) Pretend you are at a toy and game store. This time you are the parent and your child wants the latest, greatest plaything. Who would like to come to the front and show us how you would convince your child that he or she doesn't need it?

B. A WORD FROM OUR SPONSOR

1. Raise your hand if you've ever watched Saturday morning cartoons. What kinds of products are advertised at that time? Why do you think those products are advertised? Are the same products advertised at other times? When? When aren't they advertised?

2. What types of products are advertised in the evenings? During sportscasts? During soap operas? During news documentaries? Why do you think sponsors advertise certain products with certain programs?

C. CONSUMER CHARADES

1. On a piece of paper, write a career, such as farmer, waiter, teacher, or computer salesperson. (Put the papers in a bag and have a student draw a piece of paper.)

2. Without talking, act out the career that is on your paper. The rest of the class will try to guess your career.

3. (The student who guesses correctly draws a career from the bag and acts it out. This activity can also be done with consumer situations—such as grocery shopping, paying bills, and driving through a car wash—or television commercials for products—such as jeans, toys, soap, and food).

D. PHONE FUN-DAMENTALS

1. (Describe a common situation that calls for telephone use and give pairs of students a chance to role play using the phone. For example: You would like to find out the hours for swimming at the local pool.)

2. (Have students suggest other situations. Examples: You notice smoke coming out of your neighbor's window and want to notify the fire department. You need to find out the telephone number of the nearest elementary school.)

E. SPEAK OUT!

There are many times when you, as a consumer, need to stand up for your rights and speak out. Find a partner and role play each of the situations below. Remember to be polite, yet firm, about your rights!

1. You just bought a new record album. When you paid for it, the clerk gave you the wrong change. Speak out!

2. You have been patiently waiting at the bakery counter, but only the adults are being waited on. Speak out!

3. A new game you have wanted is advertised on sale in the local paper. When you go to buy it, the clerk tells you it is no longer on sale. However, the newspaper says it is. Speak out!

4. After buying a new kite, you open the package and find the sticks are missing. Go back to the store and speak out!

F. WHAT YOU "AUTO" KNOW ABOUT INSURANCE

1. (Have a brief discussion about insurance.) What is insurance? (protection that is provided through the purchase of a policy or contract) Name some different kinds of insurance. (auto, life, medical, computer, malpractice, and so on) Does everyone pay the same amount for insurance? (no) What are some factors that affect the cost of auto insurance? (age, sex, school grades, miles driven yearly, driving record, type and year of car, place of residence) Which factors can you control? (school grades, driving record, type and year of car, place of residence) Which factors can't be controlled? (age, sex)

2. Let's debate the fairness of different factors that affect the cost of auto insurance premiums.

3. (List the following on the board:)

Factors Affecting Premiums:	*Higher Premiums for:*
age	younger drivers
sex	males
school grades	poor school grades
driving record	previous auto accidents and speeding tickets
type of car and year	more expensive, new cars
place of residence	large cities

(Choose one student to stand and talk for one minute on one of the factors listed. For example, is it fair to charge higher insurance rates to younger drivers? After one minute, have another student argue the other side of the issue. At the end of the debate you might want to point out that insurance companies do not arbitrarily charge higher rates for certain groups of drivers.)

G. COMMERCIALS AND JAZZY JINGLES

1. (Turn on the radio and find a commercial, or play a tape on which you or students have recorded some commercials and jingles. See Activity 3-5, "Tune In to Feelings.")

2. Now let's listen for adjectives and how they are used. (Possible examples: "top quality," "convenient hours," "low prices," "clearance sale") Write down as many as you can.

3. How many adjectives were in the commercial? How did the adjectives affect the message?

4. (Repeat the activity by having students listen for verbs.)

H. NAME THAT SLOGAN!

1. (You or a student recites a familiar advertising slogan without naming the product associated with it. Have the class try to name the product.)

2. (After the product has been identified, discuss the following questions.) Why is this a successful slogan? Why does it stick in the consumer's mind?

3. (Repeat the activity using a different slogan.)

4. (On another day, name a product or business, such as a particular toy, cereal, restaurant, or department store. Have students make up slogans for it. List the slogans on the chalkboard and have the class vote on the best one.)

I. INTRODUCING YOU!

1. Imagine that you have a career. Introduce yourself to the group. State your name and career, and explain what you do in your job.

2. (Pair students with partners. After giving the partners a few minutes to get better acquainted with each other's careers, have students introduce their partners to the group.)

Part 2.
Application
Activities

Restaurants, Stores, and Supermarkets

Good Eating Reading   Activity 4-1

1. *Good Eating Reading*

2. *Pick a Present for a Pal*

3. *The "I Care" Game*

4. *Let Your Fingers Do the Jogging*

5. *Name, Rank, and Cereal Number*

6. *Mind Designs*

7. *Old and Neglected Ads*

8. *Supermarket B-I-M-G-O*

9. *Quick and Easy*

A. *Words for Sale*

B. *To Buy or Not to Buy*

C. *Supermarket Riddles*

D. *Catalog Sketch*

E. *Ad Appeal*

F. *International Foods*

G. *A Brand New Car*

H. *A Generic Activity*

I. *Within Reach*

You'll find a shopping cart full of ideas in this chapter. By using the marketplace as a focus for learning, you'll show students how to conduct themselves in consumer situations, how to find and analyze important information, and how to be aware of the power of advertising.

By looking at store advertisements, using the yellow pages, reading a menu, and shopping for a gift for a friend, students will develop a greater insight into real-world consumerism. Be sure to look at the Quick and Easy section for loads of instant ideas using catalogs, advertisements, and supermarket sales. You might even top off these activities with a special event by ordering pizza for a snack or taking the class on a field trip to a fast-food restaurant. (See Chapter 10 for more ideas.)

You'll find a host of reading, language, and other curricular experiences in this chapter. You don't need to shop around—the ideas are right here!

Good Eating Reading

Using menus and order forms, students do a variety of menu-related language arts activities. *(See photo, page 97.)*

Reading/Language Arts Skills: **vocabulary—compound words, words from other languages • grammar and usage—adjectives, proper nouns • study skills—dictionary • word recognition—syllables • speaking—ordering from a menu • writing—menus • spelling • handwriting • drama—role playing**

Curricular Areas: **mathematics • health • home economics • art**

Materials: **menu (page 101) • order forms (page 102) • (optional: take-out or placemat menus from local restaurants—see page 268 for other ideas)**

This breakfast buffet of appetizing activities is made to order for your students.

PREPARATION: Make a copy of the menu and fill in appropriate prices. Duplicate menus and order forms for each student.

DIRECTIONS: VERY EASY ACTIVITIES . . . As appetizers

After you've looked over your menus, we'll answer some questions. (After five minutes or so, ask questions such as the following.)

1. During what hours is breakfast served? Are the hours the same every day?

2. What is the special today?

3. How many headings are on the menu?

4. How many different beverages are available? How many different omelettes are there?

5. What items are included with the egg breakfasts?

EASY ACTIVITIES . . . To get the juices flowing

1. What compound words can you find on the menu? Is *mushroom* a compound word?

2. Make a list of adjectives used on the menu.

3. Can you find any words from languages other than English? What languages do the words come from? Use a dictionary if you're not sure.

4. Make a list of the proper nouns used on the menu.

5. Use a dictionary to find out a second way to spell the word *omelette*.

TOUGHER ACTIVITIES . . . Sink your teeth into these

1. Make a list of one-, two-, three-, four-, and five-syllable words. Which word on the menu contains the most syllables? (vegetarian)

2. Using your order form, write an order for a balanced breakfast. Be sure to include the four food groups: meats, fruits and vegetables, dairy products, and cereals. Don't forget to add up the cost of the meal.

3. Create your own omelette. Write a description of your omelette that includes a list of ingredients. Then give your omelette a name, for example, "Ava's Avocado Omelette."

4. Create your own "Today's Special."

HARD ACTIVITIES . . . To top off the meal

1. Let's practice ordering from a menu. Find a partner. One person will order a balanced breakfast while the other takes the order and writes it on the order form. Switch places with your partner so that each of you has a chance to order and to take an order.

2. After you have practiced ordering breakfast, pretend that you are dissatisfied with part of the meal. Role play telling the waiter or waitress that you are unhappy with the meal.

3. Design your own menu. Be sure to include item names, descriptive words when appropriate, and prices.

VARIATION:

(See *Kids Are Consumers, Too! Real-World Mathematics for Today's Classroom*, "Menu Math," page 139.)

Breakfast served
6am.-11am. Mon.-Fri.
7a.m.-1pm. Sat.+Sun.

BREAKFAST

TODAY'S SPECIAL
Avocado Omelette
3-egg omelette with cheese, served with hash browns and toast, muffins, or biscuits.
$.

EGG BREAKFASTS

Cooked "egg-zactly" the way you like them by "eggs-perts." Breakfasts include hash browns and toast, muffins, or biscuits.

2 EGGS . . . .$.

ASPARAGUS and EGGS . . . . $.

HAM and EGGS . . . .$.

STEAK and EGGS . . . . .$.

EGGS BENEDICT . . . . .$.

EGGS ARNOLD . . . . . .$.

PANCAKES

SHORT STACK . . . . . .$.

TALL STACK . . . . . .$.

PEACH PANCAKES . . . .$.

SIDE ORDERS

FRESH FRUIT IN SEASON.$.

WHEAT TOAST. . . . . .$.

BISCUITS and GRAVY . . .$.

ENGLISH MUFFIN . . . .$.

HOT OATMEAL . . . . . .$.

COLD CEREAL WITH MILK.$.

BEVERAGES

COFFEE	.	ORANGE JUICE	.
TEA	.	TOMATO JUICE	.
MILK	.	CARROT JUICE	.

OMELETTES

Our "egg-ceptional" 3-egg omelette breakfasts include hash browns and toast, muffins, or biscuits.

PLAIN . . . .$.

CHEESE . . . .$.
   Made with your choice of Jack, American, or Cheddar cheese.

DENVER . . . .$.
   Made with bell pepper, onions, and ham.

SANTA MARIA . . . .$.
   Made with BBQ beans and 2 types of cheese.

VEGETARIAN . . . .$.
   Made with onions, broccoli, green peppers, mushrooms, and your choice of cheese.

"EGG-STRAS" $.
   Cheese . . . . $.
   Olives . . . .$.
   Shrimp. . . . .$.
   Avocado . . . .$.
   Onions. . . . .$.
   Peanut Butter . . .$.

HUEVOS RANCHEROS

3 scrambled eggs topped with cheese and salsa and served with beans, rice, and corn tortillas . . . .$.

NAME:

ORDER:

TOTAL:

NAME:

ORDER:

TOTAL:

Pick a Present
for a Pal

Students, in groups of three or four, choose at least one item from a catalog for each member of the group. Then they fill out order forms for the items.

Reading/Language Arts Skills: **study skills—catalogs, order forms, index • spelling • handwriting**

Curricular Areas: **mathematics • home economics**

Materials: **catalogs (or page 105) • catalog order forms (from catalogs or page 106) • gift certificate (page 107) • (optional: calculators)**

Price is no object as students enjoy a catalog shopping spree.

PREPARATION: Make a copy of the catalog page and fill in appropriate prices. Duplicate a catalog page, an order form, and a gift certificate for each student.

DISCUSSION: How is ordering from a catalog similar to buying in a department store? How is it different?

DIRECTIONS:
1. Divide students into groups of three or four, or let them choose their own groups.
2. This is "Pick a Present for Your Pal Day." Each of you will have a chance to order a gift for each person in your group.
3. Before you start selecting wonderful gifts, let's review the information that's needed on the catalog order form: date, name and address, item name, quantity, catalog number, page number, color, size, item price, and total price.
4. Look through your catalogs for items you think your friends would like. Ask them for suggestions, too. Use the catalog index to help you locate items. (See page 15 for catalog index activity.)
5. Each time you find something you want to order for someone in your group, fill in one line on the order blank.
6. When your group members have finished ordering gifts for each other, fill in the top of your gift certificate card with your name. Pass it to the members of your group so that they can list the gifts they ordered for you.

VARIATIONS:
1. Students may enjoy ordering items from the catalog to make the classroom more comfortable, attractive, and functional.
2. Using a microcomputer database program, have students design their own catalog order forms.

School & Office Supplies

Pencils . . . . $. ea.
Colored pencils (box of 6) $.
Crayons (box of 16) . . . . . . $.
Markers . . . . $. ea.
Florescent markers . . . . . . $. ea.

Spiral notebook . . . . $.
3-ring binder . . . . $.
Notebook paper . . . . $.
Folders . . . . $.
Book covers:
    Plain . . . . $.
    Designer . . . . $.
    Furry . . . . $.

Erasers:
    Pencil top . . . . $.
    Star . . . . $.
    Rainbow . . . . $.
Pencil Tops:
    Animal . . . . $.
    Nameplates . . . . $.
    Furry . . . . $.

Calculators
    Battery-powered . . . . $.
    Solar-powered . . . . $.

Pencil holder . . . . $.
Desk organizer . . . . $.
Desk nameplate . . . . $.
Desk lamp . . . . $.
Desk flashlight . . . . $.
Seat cushion . . . . $.

Briefcases
    Standard . . . . $.
    With calculator . . . . $.

Catalog Order Form
(Use for Activity 4-2.)

CATALOG ORDER FORM

DATE OF ORDER: _____

SHIP TO:

BILL TO:

Name _____

Name _____

Address _____

Address _____

City _____

City _____

State _____ Zip Code _____ Office Use _____

State _____ Zip Code _____ Office Use _____

Page	Item Number	How Many	Name of Item	Color	Size	Price Each	Total Price

Total for Goods _____

Tax _____

Total _____

MAIL ORDER TO:

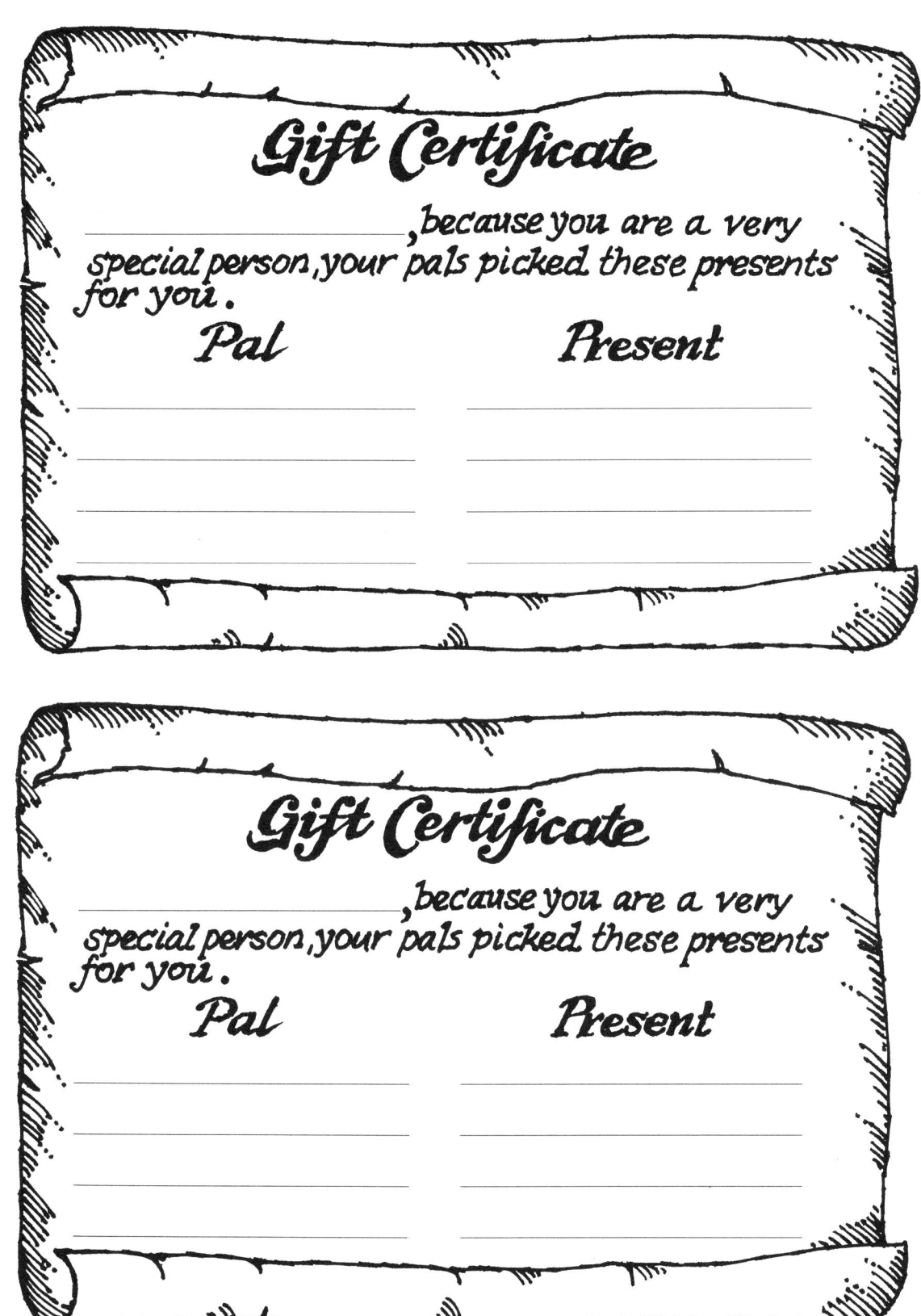

Gift Certificate

_____, because you are a very
special person, your pals picked these presents
for you.

Pal   **Present**

Gift Certificate

_____, because you are a very
special person, your pals picked these presents
for you.

Pal   **Present**

The "I Care" Game

In this game, players spend money for gifts and greetings to send to friends and family.

Reading/Language Arts Skills: **comprehension—following directions • handwriting • spelling**

Curricular Areas: **mathematics**

Materials: **game board (page 277) • game spinner (page 276) • paper clip and pencil • playing piece for each student (a coin, ring, or button) • notebook paper • (optional: calculators)**

There are many ways to communicate the message that you care about someone. Here's a game that gives kids a chance to buy different kinds of items to express their feelings.

PREPARATION: To make tally sheet:

Have students mark off two columns on a piece of notebook paper. Tell them to label the columns *Item* and *Amount* and then put a starting amount of money (such as $200) at the top of the *Amount* column.

To make spinner:

1. Duplicate game spinner on page 276. (You will need one spinner for each group of players.)
2. Fill in the five sections with the numbers 1, 2, 3, 4, 5.

To make game board:

1. You or your students can fill in the following information on the game board (page 277).

A. Fill in circle blanks with:
   - GIVE $10 TO THE NURSING HOME
   - GIVE $20 TO HANDICAPPED CHILDREN
   - SEND $15 TO THE HEART FUND

B. Fill in diamond blanks with:
   - SEND YOUR COUSIN $10
   - SEND GRANDMA $25
   - SEND YOUR UNCLE $15

C. Fill in the remaining 20 spaces with the names of gifts or greetings and a reasonable price for each item. Use items such as:

• GREETING CARD	$ _____
• TELEGRAM	$ _____
• BIRTHDAY CARD	$ _____
• PUZZLE	$ _____
• BOOK	$ _____
• PAIR OF SOCKS	$ _____
• PHONE CALL	$ _____
• SINGING TELEGRAM	$ _____
• GAME	$ _____
• STUFFED ANIMAL	$ _____
• GOLDFISH	$ _____
• FLOWERS	$ _____

SEND GRANDMA $25   GOLDFISH $2   GREETING CARD $1.25   SEND $15 TO THE HEART FUND

2. Duplicate a completed game board for each group of students. (Larger boards can be made by making a transparency and tracing around a projected image on tag board or stiffening fabric used for interfacing.)

DIRECTIONS:

1. Players spin to determine which player will go first. The player with the highest number spins again and moves the number of spaces indicated.

2. Play continues to the left. For each turn, a player spins and moves. As each player lands on a space, the information is read, the item and amount are recorded on the tally sheet, and the amount is subtracted from the running balance. (This subtraction can be performed using a calculator.)

3. Continue until all players reach the finish line. The winner is the most generous player with the least amount of money remaining. It's obvious the winner really cares!

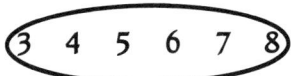
Let Your Fingers Do the Jogging

Using a sample yellow page from the telephone book, students do a variety of language-related activities.

Reading/Language Arts Skills: **study skills—alphabetical order, telephone books • grammar and usage—adjectives, sentences • vocabulary—compound words, abbreviations • writing—business letters, codes, messages • critical thinking—evaluating advertisements • speaking—using the telephone • drama—role playing**

Curricular Areas: **mathematics • art**

Materials: **phone book yellow page (page 113) • telephone message forms (page 77) • (optional: copy of actual phone book yellow page)**

Your students will warm up to this complete mental workout as they jog through the yellow pages.

PREPARATION: Make a copy of the phone book page (page 113) and telephone message forms (page 77) for each student. You might want to run copies on yellow paper.

DIRECTIONS: VERY EASY ACTIVITIES . . . To stretch the mind

After you've looked over the telephone book yellow page, we'll answer some questions. (After a few minutes, ask questions such as the following:)

1. What is the heading on the page?

2. How many sporting goods stores are listed? How many sportswear stores?

3. Which store has two locations?

4. Which stores have backpacking equipment? Ski rental?

5. Would this page be found near the beginning, middle, or end of the yellow pages? How can you tell?

6. Which stores would you call to order team uniforms for your school?

EASY ACTIVITIES . . . At an easy pace

1. Put the items available at Good Sport Sporting Goods in alphabetical order.

2. List the adjectives found on this page.

3. Make a list of compound words from this page.

4. Are there any abbreviations on the page? What are they? What do they stand for?

TOUGHER ACTIVITIES . . . To give the mind a total workout

1. This yellow page is from the town where your twenty-four-year-old brother or sister lives. It is far away from your home. Write a letter to a store to order a present for your brother or sister. Find out how your gift will be delivered, what the delivery charges will be, whether there is any sales tax, and so on. Be sure to use complete sentences. (A word processor would be helpful for this activity.)

2. Choose three stores from this page. Write a word phone number for each (see Activity 2-6, "Dial M-Y P-H-O-N-E Number," page 57).

3. Which ad on this page do you think is the most eye catching? Explain why.

4. Redesign one of the ads on this page.

5. Design a phone book ad for your own business (see Activity 5-3, "Now You're in Business!" page 137).

CULMINATING ACTIVITY . . . As a cool down at the finish line

With a partner, role play phoning various stores from this page to find out the following information:

> How much does a letter jacket cost?
> What hours is the store open?
> Does the store carry badminton equipment?
> Is the store accepting job applications?

Take turns calling and answering the calls. Use the telephone message forms (page 77) to write down the information you get when you call.

S 610 Sporting-Sportswear

Sporting Goods-Dealers (Cont'd)

BARNEY'S

THE ULTIMATE SPORTS SHOP

- Active Sportswear
- Camping and Backpacking Equipment
- Athletic Footwear
- Flying Disks
- Ski Rentals and Accessories

OPEN 6 DAYS
Mon.-Sat.

400 W. Health Ln.
805 227-6397

GOOD SPORT SPORTING GOODS

923 Fairplay Ct.
Teamfield

- Athletic Shoes
- Water Skis
- Swimwear
- Shoes
- Backpacking
- Camping
- Sports Apparel
- Tennis Equipment
- Skates

COMPARE OUR PRICES
437-7678
OPEN 7 DAYS

Centerfield

Sporting Goods

- Baseball
- Football
- Basketball
- Swimming
- Aerobic Wear
- Running
- Weights

2 LOCATIONS TO SERVE YOU

643 Fastpitch Ln.	121 Grandslam Ave.
378-7824	476-3756

GONE FISHING
923 Angler St. 347-4464
Please See Advertisement This Page

GOOD SPORT SPORTING GOODS 437-7678
Please See Advertisement This Page

SPORT STOP
2468 Fieldgoal Ln. 777-8787
Please See Advertisement This Page

Sportswear-Retail

CALL
777-8787

TEAM SPORT SPECIALIST

Team Order Discounts
All High School
Letter Jackets Available
2468 Fieldgoal Ln.

Club Wawona
Sportswear

292-9662

A complete line of sport
and swimwear for men,
women, and children

203 WAWONA AVE.

GONE FISHING

THE FINEST SELECTION OF CAMPING AND SPORTFISHING EQUIPMENT IN THE COUNTY

9:30-6:00
Mon.-Sat.
9-5 Sun.

347-4464

923 Angler St.

ACME ACTIVE WEAR

222-8483

Footwear
Beachwear
Team Uniforms
Leisure Wear

463 W. Health Ln.

SNAPPY CAPS

Official Caps
for all major-league
baseball teams

762-7227

263 Grandslam Ave.

Name, Rank, and Cereal Number

This learning station consists of a set of Task Cards and a collection of empty cereal boxes. Students do reading and writing activities based on information found on the boxes.

Reading/Language Arts Skills: comprehension—classifying • grammar and usage—adjectives, sentences • critical thinking—comparing and contrasting • study skills—alphabetical order • vocabulary—abbreviations • writing—business letters, commercials • mechanics of writing—capitalization, punctuation • spelling • handwriting

Curricular Areas: mathematics • health • home economics • art

Materials: Task Cards 1-11 (pages 117 to 120) • a variety of empty cereal boxes • tape recorder and cassette • (optional: cereal box front, back, and sides, pages 9, 10, and 11)

There's nothing like reading a cereal box over breakfast. Here's a chance for kids to catch up on the latest news from the cereal companies—and to practice reading and writing skills at the same time.

PREPARATION: Duplicate a set of Task Cards 1-11 (to make them last longer, laminate the Task Cards or cover them with clear contact paper). Make a learning station that includes at least five empty cereal boxes and the Task Cards. (The Task Cards can be kept inside the cereal boxes for convenient storage and student use.)

DIRECTIONS: (You can use these eleven Task Cards as lessons for the whole class, or you can set them up as activities for a learning station.)

VARIATION: As a math activity, Task Cards can be made to emphasize math skills. For example:

1. List the number of grams of cereal and servings contained in each box.

2. Find the price on each box. Put the prices in order from lowest to highest.

3. Compare the weight listed on the boxes. Rank them in order from lightest to heaviest.

4. Compare the expiration dates on the boxes. Rank them in order.

5. Choose two boxes. Calculate the difference in calories per serving for each cereal. Do the same for protein, carbohydrate, fat, and sodium.

Name, Rank, and Cereal Number

(Use with Activity 4-5)

Choose one cereal box. Divide your paper in half. Write *Useful Information* at the top of one half and *Unimportant Information* at the top of the other half. Find examples of each type of information on the cereal box and list them in the appropriate column.

Name, Rank, and Cereal Number

(Use with Activity 4-5)

Choose two cereal boxes. On your paper, list the adjectives used on each box to make the product sound appealing to the shopper.

Name, Rank, and Cereal Number

(Use with Activity 4-5)

On food packages, ingredients are listed in order according to amount. The main ingredient is listed first. Choose two cereal boxes. For each one, list the main ingredient as well as the ingredient used in the smallest amount.

Name, Rank, and Cereal Number

(Use with Activity 4-5)

Select one cereal box. Write the brand name at the top of your paper. Find all the different times the name of the cereal appears on the box. Copy each one, using the same style of writing that is used on the box—bold type, colorful writing, italics, and so on.

Write a short paragraph explaining why the name is written several times and in different ways.

Name, Rank, and Cereal Number

(Use with Activity 4-5)

Choose one cereal box. Find the nutrients listed under Percentage of U.S. Recommended Daily Allowances (U.S. RDA). Put the list of nutrients in alphabetical order.

Name, Rank, and Cereal Number

(Use with Activity 4-5)

Select one cereal box. List all of the abbreviations printed on the box. Beside each abbreviation write the word or words it stands for.

Name, Rank, and Cereal Number

(Use with Activity 4-5)

Choose two cereal boxes. Based on the packaging, which cereal would you be most likely to buy? Write a paragraph that tells what information on the package influenced your decision.

Name, Rank, and Cereal Number

(Use with Activity 4-5)

Select one box and create a radio commercial for that cereal. Write the commercial, then record it on a tape recorder. Play it back and listen to your cereal commercial. Share the commercial with the class.

Name, Rank, and Cereal Number

(Use with Activity 4-5)

Select one cereal box. Imagine that you are an executive in charge of product development for one of the cereals. Lately your sales have dropped. Your job is to improve the cereal to promote sales. Change the shape of the cereal, add a tasty new ingredient, redesign the box, create a new slogan, and so on. Explain your changes in a letter to the board of directors. Be sure to express your ideas clearly in complete sentences and use correct spelling, capitalization, and punctuation.

Name, Rank, and Cereal Number

(Use with Activity 4-5)

Choose one cereal box. Read and compare the top flap of the box and the bottom flap. In your comparison, list the similarities and differences. Choose another cereal box and repeat the procedure. What do both boxes (top and bottom flaps) have in common? How are they different?

Name, Rank, and Cereal Number

(Use with Activity 4-5)

Choose a cereal box with a guarantee. Imagine you are satisfied or dissatisfied with the product. Write a letter to the company explaining what you like about the cereal or why you are not happy with it. Use complete sentences, and be sure to remind them of the stated guarantee!

Mind Designs

Students analyze stores and shops to develop an awareness of how interior decorating and window displays affect consumer attitudes. Then they write an essay about how they would decorate the "ultimate" shop to attract consumers.

Reading/Language Arts Skills: **critical thinking—comparing and contrasting, classifying • writing—essays • grammar and usage—sentences • mechanics of writing—capitalization, punctuation • creative expression**

Curricular Areas: **mathematics • home economics • art**

Materials: **paper • pencils**

Display these essays in your classroom for open house and watch the parents' surprise at how consumer-wise their kids have become!

DISCUSSION: What are some ways stores are decorated to appeal to shoppers? (color of paint on walls, furniture used for displays, interesting objects and fad items on display, and so on) Does music playing in the shop affect the atmosphere? In what way?

DIRECTIONS:

1. Think of one of your favorite stores or shops. Imagine you are entering the shop and then browsing around. Be very aware of the total environment and why you like being in that shop. Make a list of things used to create the shop's decor and atmosphere.

2. Classify your findings into the following categories: colors, textures, designs, music, furniture, wall decorations, and miscellaneous objects.

3. Look at your categorized list of decor items. From the list, circle the things that most influence you to shop at this store.

4. Using the circled items along with your own ideas for decorating, write a short essay explaining how *you* would design and decorate a shop to appeal to people your age. Include in your essay the reasons why you chose to decorate the shop as you did. Be sure to use complete sentences and correct spelling, capitalization, and punctuation. If you like, draw a picture or diagram to illustrate your essay.

VARIATIONS:

1. Have students use a word processor to compose their essays.

2. Take the class to a local shopping mall for a field trip. Give each student a copy of the directions to use as a checklist.

3. Using a database program, have students list and categorize information about the decor of several shops. Encourage them to compare the features of these shops.

Old and Neglected Ads

Students find antonyms for the adjectives used in magazine ads and then redesign the ad to match the changed message.

Reading/Language Arts Skills: **grammar and usage—adjectives • critical thinking—evaluating advertisements, expressing opinions • creative expression • vocabulary—antonyms**

Curricular Areas: **art • social studies**

Materials: **magazines • drawing paper • scissors • glue or paste • crayons or markers**

Would you buy a product that was old and neglected? The adjectives used in ads may have more of an influence on us than we think.

DISCUSSION: What is an adjective? (a word that modifies, or describes, a noun) What are some common adjectives used in advertising? (*new, improved, natural, refreshing*, and so on) Why do advertisements use so many adjectives? (to make the product sound appealing) Do the adjectives always give you valid information about the product?

DIRECTIONS: 1. Today we will look at how the adjectives used in ads can influence our decision to buy the product. (Pass out magazines.) Please look through your magazine and find an ad that contains several adjectives. Cut it out.

2. What are some of the adjectives used in the ad you chose? (possible examples: amazing, improved, daring, bouncy) What are some antonyms for these adjectives? (predictable, neglected, cowardly, limp)

3. Change the message in your ad by changing each adjective to a word with the opposite meaning. On your drawing paper, redesign the ad to match the new message.

4. Let's share some of our ads. (Choose students to come to the front of the room and hold up both the magazine ad and their changed version.) How has the message been changed? Which ad sounds more appealing? Would you consider buying the product in the ad you rewrote? How are we influenced by adjectives in ads?

Supermarket B-I-M-G-O

This game is a modified version of bingo. Students make their own B-I-M-G-O cards, using items found in their local supermarkets.

Reading/Language Arts Skills: vocabulary—content area words • critical thinking—classifying • spelling

Curricular Areas: home economics

Materials: **B-I-M-G-O Card (page 125)** • **two game spinners (page 276)** • **paper clips and pencils** • **15 markers for each student (beans, coins, or buttons)**

Make this game in one session—and play it all year!

PREPARATION: To make spinners:

1. Duplicate two game spinners (page 276).

2. On one spinner, fill in the five sections with the words *Bakery, Dairy, Meat & Fish, Grocery, Produce.*

3. On the other spinner, fill in each of the five sections with a different letter (for example, *C, D, E, F,* and *G*).

To make B-I-M-G-O cards:

1. Duplicate one B-I-M-G-O card (page 125) for each student. Have them read the names of the supermarket sections at the top of the card.

2. Students write the name of an item from the supermarket in each space on the card. All the items must start with one of the five letters chosen for the spinner. Tell students to be sure to put each item in the appropriate column.

BAKERY	DA**I**RY	**M**EAT & Fish	**G**ROCERY	PR**O**DUCE
Corn Bread	Cherry Yogurt	Fish	Granola Bars	Eggplant
Fruit Pie	Goat Cheese	Chicken	Egg Noodles	Dried Fruit

DIRECTIONS:

1. (Decide who will be the B-I-M-G-O Manager.) The Manager spins both spinners and calls out the results. She or he names the column, then the letter. For example, "Grocery, starting with C."

2. Players may cover *only one* space that fits the column and letter. For example, they could cover *catsup* or *corn tortillas* in the grocery column, but not both.

3. When a player covers five spaces in a row—horizontally, vertically, or diagonally—he or she calls out, "B-I-M-G-O!"

B-I-M-G-O Card
(Use for Activity 4-8)

Bakery	daIry	Meat & Fish	Grocery	prOduce

Quick and Easy

A. WORDS FOR SALE

1. (Write on the chalkboard the name of a store in your town—for example, *David's Department Store.*)

2. Using the letters in this name, find words that name things you could buy at that store. (*diapers, tires, tents, paint, ovens, stamps, darts,* and so on)

3. (On another day:) Let's make a list of items that start with the letters in the store's name. (*dishes, atlas, vitamins, ink pad, dolls,* and so on)

B. TO BUY OR NOT TO BUY

1. What are some sources of information that influence what products you buy? (friends, parents, TV and radio commercials, magazine ads, window displays, billboards, sale ads)

2. (List student responses on the chalkboard.) Look at the list on the chalkboard. Which of these factors is most likely to influence your choice when you buy a record or cassette (a pair of jeans, sports equipment, a hamburger)? Write your answer on scrap paper.

3. (Read the list from the chalkboard. Have students raise their hands as you read the factor that influences them most. Write the total for each response on the chalkboard.)

4. What are the implications of these buying factors for businesses and advertisers?

C. SUPERMARKET RIDDLES

1. I'm thinking of something that comes in a carton. The carton says, "99 cents" and "Contents—1 dozen." What might it be? (eggs)

2. Down the paper products aisle are packages that say, "72 sq ft total area, 90 sheets, two-ply, 11 in. × 10.6 in." What are they? (paper towels)

3. These are packaged in 5- or 10-pound bags. What are they if they have eyes but can't see? (potatoes) What if they have a colorful name and like to be squeezed? (oranges) What if they add fuel to a fire? (charcoal) This item is a homonym for what a rose, a daisy, or a tulip is? (flour)

4. (Have students make up more riddles to challenge the class.)

D. CATALOG SKETCH

1. (Name an item you can buy in a catalog.) I am going to order a camera from a catalog. List three accessories that could go with my camera. (Camera strap, case, extra lens)

2. Now sketch out a catalog page that displays these items. Your page should include catalog numbers, sizes, colors, and prices.

E. AD APPEAL

1. Many magazine advertisements appeal to one or more of the five senses: sight, taste, smell, touch, and hearing.

2. (Show the class an advertisement from a magazine or newspaper.) What senses are appealed to in this ad? What key words or phrases are used to create the appeal? (spices, rich, mellow, mouth-watering, creamy, and so on)

F. INTERNATIONAL FOODS

1. Many foods in the supermarket come from other countries. Make a list of international foods and the countries they come from.

2. (Encourage students to ask parents about international foods that were available when they were children.)

G. A BRAND NEW CAR

1. (On the chalkboard, make a chart with the following categories of car buyers in a column on the left side of the chart: college student, small family, traveling salesperson, professional basketball player, large family. Students make the same chart on lined paper at their desks.)

2. What things are people concerned with when selecting a new car? (gas mileage, style, roominess, dependability, price, and so on) List these concerns across the top of your chart.

3. Which car buyers would be most concerned with gas mileage? Put check marks in the gas mileage column for those categories of buyers. (Have students complete the chart by checking off the appropriate concerns for each category of car buyer.)

H. A GENERIC ACTIVITY

1. (Hold up two brands of the same grocery item, one a nationally advertised brand, the other a generic brand. Discuss the influence of packaging and advertising.)

2. Which product is less expensive? What might influence the cost of each product? (packaging, advertising)

3. Do you think these two products are of the same quality? How could you find out?

4. Which product would you buy? Why?

I. WITHIN REACH

1. Make a list of products you think might be found on low supermarket shelves where small children can see or reach them. Why do you think these items would be placed on low shelves?

2. Make a list of items that might be found on shelves next to the checkout line. Why do you think these are called "impulse" items?

Careers, Jobs, and Chores

Career Connection—The Interview   Activity 5-4

1. *Career Pursuit*
2. *Patent Pending*
3. *Now You're in Business!*
4. *Career Connection—The Interview*
5. *Apply Yourself—Get a Job!*
6. *Step to Success—Write a Résumé*
7. *Classroom Chores—A Problem?*
8. *Plan Ahead*
9. *Quick and Easy*

A. *Making Mad Money*
B. *Who Works Here?*
C. *I'm Thinking of a Career*
D. *Creative Licenses*
E. *101 Uses*
F. *You're the Boss!*
G. *Job Search*
H. *Baby Sitter's Idea Kit*
I. *Job Skills*

Did you want to be a teacher when you grew up? Did you like to play school? We did! But we also liked to play firefighter, doctor, farmer, movie star, and singing waiter!

It's important for kids to dream about the careers and jobs they might have when they grow up. But preparing for a career requires more than dreaming; it requires hard work and careful planning.

The activities in this chapter put your students to work in the world of language arts. Students have a chance to design their own businesses, fill out job applications, write résumés, talk about chores, and interview parents and other community members about the world of work. We've also included a game in which students look at the many career opportunities available to tomorrow's adults.

By the way, you might want to take a look at some of the career-related projects in Chapter 8. These projects, along with the activities found here, are sure to start students thinking about careers and jobs they can do today—as well as get them to look ahead to the challenges they may face in the future.

Career Pursuit

In groups of three to five, players spin a letter of the alphabet. For each spin, they list the names of careers that begin with that letter.

Reading/Language Arts Skills: vocabulary—content area words • spelling • critical thinking—comparing and contrasting, classifying

Curricular Areas: social studies

Materials: game spinner (page 276) • paper clip and pencil • writing paper • timer or a clock with a second hand

---

Put students' minds to work with a flick of the spinner!

PREPARATION: To make spinner:

1. Duplicate a game spinner (page 276) for each group of three to five players.

2. Divide each section of the spinner in half so that there are ten sections. Write a different letter of the alphabet in each section.

DIRECTIONS:

1. (Choose one player to be in charge of the timer. Every player needs paper and a pencil.)

2. The youngest player spins the spinner. As the paper clip lands on a letter, the timekeeper sets the timer for three minutes. (Time may vary.)

3. Players list the names of as many careers as they can think of that start with the letter indicated on the spinner before the time runs out. (For example, *L* = lumberjack, lifeguard, locksmith, legal secretary, librarian, and so on.) Players read their lists and get one point for each career listed.

4. The second youngest player spins, and the game continues. If the same letter is spun, players must list different careers.

5. The game can end at any time. The winner is the player with the highest point total.

VARIATIONS:

1. Players take turns spinning. As the clip lands on a letter, each player, taking turns, names an occupation that starts with that letter. Occupations may not be repeated. When a player can't come up with an occupation that hasn't already been named, he or she drops out. The last remaining player is the winner.

2. Have students discuss the similarities and differences among the careers they have listed. Then have them think of ways to sort the careers into categories.

Patent Pending

Students design and patent a device to perform a simple household chore. They draw a diagram of the invention and write a short explanation of how it operates.

Reading/Language Arts Skills: **critical thinking—analyzing cause and effect • creative expression • study skills—diagrams • writing—explanatory paragraphs • grammar and usage—sentences • spelling**

Curricular Areas: **science • social studies • art • home economics**

Materials: **Inventor's Oath form and Patent Certificate (page 135) • writing paper • drawing paper • crayons or markers**

These inventions just might revolutionize household chores!

PREPARATION: Duplicate the Inventors' Oath form and the Patent Certificate (page 135) for each student. Select four or five students to be patent officers. These students will decide whether or not the inventions submitted meet patent criteria.

DISCUSSION: What is a patent? (a document that grants the exclusive right to make and sell an invention or process) Today you will be inventors. You will design a new appliance to help you do a household chore, and then you will submit your plan to the patent office.

The patent office requires that three documents be submitted when applying for a patent: a written description of the invention, a diagram, and a signed and witnessed oath declaring that you are the first and original inventor.

DIRECTIONS:
1. Think of some of the household chores you do by hand. (making beds, feeding pets, taking out the trash, emptying the dishwasher, dusting, washing windows, and so on) Decide on a chore that you would like to have help with.

2. Design an appliance that might help you with the chore you have chosen. Draw a diagram of it and label the important parts—on and off switches, attachments, cords, pulleys, gears, and so on.

3. Write a full description of your appliance. Include the chore it performs, how it works, and directions for its use. Be sure to write in complete sentences and check your spelling.

4. Submit your diagram and description to the patent office along with the signed and witnessed Inventor's Oath. (You may want to have a box or folder labeled "Patent Pending" so that students have a place to submit completed inventions.)

5. (Patent officers will check inventions to make sure they meet patent criteria and then will issue official patent certificates.)

INVENTOR'S OATH

I hereby declare that I am the first and original inventor of this device. Signed and witnessed this _____ day of _____, 19____.

_____   _____
Signature of Inventor   Witness

PATENT CERTIFICATE

This certificate is presented to:

_____

as first and original inventor of

_____.

Presented this _____ day of _____, 19____.

_____
Signature of Patent Officer

_____
Patent #

OFFICIAL PATENT SEAL

Now You're in Business!

Students decide on jobs they can do and then prepare to set themselves up in business.

Reading/Language Arts Skills: **creative expression • writing—business fliers, advertisements • spelling • drama • listening—critical listening • speaking—using the telephone**

Curricular Areas: **social studies**

Materials: **paper • markers • scissors • (optional: sample business cards • tape recorder and blank tape • VCR, video camera, and tape • television)**

Kids are always wanting to earn money. With this activity and a little imagination, they're in business!

DISCUSSION: What are some jobs a person your age could do? (gardening, baby sitting, house cleaning, delivering newspapers, walking dogs, and so on) (Write students' responses on the chalkboard.) What might you need in order to do some of these jobs? (gardening equipment, transportation to baby's home, cleaning supplies, bicycle, and so on) (For additional ideas, see "Let's Form a Job Club," Project 8-4.)

DIRECTIONS: 1. (Students can work alone or in groups to choose a job they really can do.) List the reasons why you are qualified to do this job or to perform this service.

2. Do one or more of the following activities:

    A. FLIER: Design a business flier. Include your name, the service you offer, and how you can be contacted. (Students can use the following sample design. It has strips at the bottom for interested customers to tear off.)

Cut up from bottom to create strips that can be torn off.

B. BUSINESS CARD: Design a business card. (Optional: Show students sample cards.) Be sure to include your service, name, and telephone number.

C. RADIO ADVERTISEMENT: Write a short radio advertisement for your business. Record it on a tape recorder and then listen to your ad. You may want to redo it and make changes in your tone of voice, rate of speaking, and so on. Listen again. When you have it just right, let your class radio audience hear it. (Some communities offer free radio spots for youth announcements.)

D. TV ADVERTISEMENT: Write a TV commercial for your business. Practice it in front of several classmates. Ask them for suggestions and revise it accordingly. Perform it for the entire class. (Optional: Videotape the commercial and then play it for the class.)

E. TELEPHONE ROLE PLAY: Choose a friend to act as a person interested in your product or service. Role play a telephone call in response to your advertisement. Your friend can ask questions about your service, and you can answer them.

F. (For additional experience in business, see "Let's Advertise Nationwide," Project 8-2, page 213.)

Career Connection—
The Interview

Students invite workers from the community to the classroom, or contact them by phone, and interview them about their careers. *(See photo, page 131.)*

Reading/Language Arts Skills:	**writing—invitations, descriptive paragraphs, thank-you notes • drama—role playing • speaking—interviewing, using the telephone • listening—listening for information**
Curricular Areas:	**social studies**
Materials:	**(optional: tape recorder and blank cassette • camera or VCR, video camera, and television)**

This activity does a great job of putting your students' natural curiosity to work.

PREPARATION:

1. Invite parents or other community members to class to talk about their jobs. Handmade invitations may be used. (See Activity 7-1, "Greeting Cards—Say It with Style," page 181.)

2. If you plan to tape the interview, ask the speaker's permission in advance.

DIRECTIONS:

(Preparing for the interview:)

1. Tomorrow we will be interviewing a pediatrician (firefighter, letter carrier, and so on). What are some of the things you would like to ask that person about his or her job? (education needed, work hours, typical day's events, job responsibilities, and so on)

2. Please write five questions you would like to ask during the interview. Number each question and leave at least two lines between each one to record the answers.

3. (After questions have been written, choose students to role play the interview.) I'll be the pediatrician for now. Who would like to practice asking me an interview question?

(During the interview:)

1. (You may wish to go over group interview procedures before beginning.) What are some things you should keep in mind while conducting this interview? (raise your hand to ask a question, stand when addressing the person being interviewed, thank the speaker for answering your question, speak clearly, listen carefully)

3. (You or a student can introduce your guest and provide time for him or her to make some opening comments.) Let's begin the interview. Raise your hand if you have a question for our guest.

4. (The length of the interview will vary depending on the amount of time your guest has and the attention span of the students.)

(After the interview:)

1. Please use your interview questions and answers to write a paragraph describing the job of our guest. Include interesting facts you have just learned about the job. (If the interview was taped, students can use the tape to help them.)

2. (Be sure to send a thank-you note to your guest. This can be written by one student or by the whole class. For card ideas, see Activity 7-1, "Greeting Cards—Say It with Style," page 181.)

3. (On another day, if the interview was taped:) We're going to play the interview tape. Listen for these things: Are the questions and answers clear and understandable? Do the interviewers and the speaker keep to the topic?

VARIATIONS:

1. Have students contact community workers on the phone to set up an appointment for a telephone interview or an interview at that person's place of business.

2. For more information on conducting and critiquing interviews, see Project 8-5, "Career Day," page 226.

Apply Yourself— Get a Job!

Students fill out job applications.

Reading/Language Arts Skills: **study skills—job applications • comprehension—following directions • spelling**

Curricular Areas: **social studies**

Materials: **Job Application form (page 143)**

You'll learn more about your students as they apply themselves to this activity.

DISCUSSION: What are some of the tasks involved in looking for a job? (looking in the help-wanted ads, making phone calls, filling out a job application, going for an interview) Today we will work on one of these tasks—filling out a job application. Why is it important to do a neat, accurate job when filling out an application? (The prospective employer gets a first impression of the applicant from the application.)

DIRECTIONS: 1. (Have students fill out the Job Application form, page 143.)

2. (For students with no work history:) What are some of the chores you do at home? (baby-sitting, caring for pets, yardwork, planning and cooking meals, housecleaning, laundry, and so on) How about at school? (chalkboard monitor, paper monitor, lunch count, playground cleanup) These chores can be written in as part of your work history.

Job Application Form
(Use for Activity 5-5)

PITTS-BURGERS

JOB APPLICATION

An Equal Opportunity Employer

PLEASE PRINT

TODAY'S DATE	NAME (FIRST, MIDDLE, LAST)	SOCIAL SECURITY NO.	PHONE NO.

ADDRESS (NUMBER, STREET, CITY, STATE, AND ZIP)	IN EMERGENCY, NOTIFY (NAME, ADDRESS)	PHONE NO.

SCHOOL ATTENDING, CITY, STATE	GRADE	EXTRA-CURRICULAR ACTIVITIES

WORK HISTORY

Enter below your last two positions held. Start with the most recent; include any volunteer experience.

Dates From	Through	Company Name and Address	Position Held	Reason for Leaving

DETAILS OF WORK WANTED

For what job are you applying?	Part Time ☐ Full Time ☐	Hours Available	SUN.	MON.	TUES.	WED.	THURS.	FRI.	SAT.

REFERENCES: PLEASE LIST THE NAMES OF THREE PEOPLE WHO HAVE KNOWN YOU FOR AT LEAST ONE YEAR (EXCLUDING RELATIVES).

NAME	RELATIONSHIP	PHONE NO.	COMMENTS (FOR OFFICE USE ONLY)

Please add your signature in the space provided.

Signature _____ Date _____

THANK YOU FOR YOUR TIME AND EFFORT AND FOR YOUR INTEREST IN WORKING AT PITTS-BURGERS.

Step to Success—
Write a Résumé

Students explore help-wanted ads, select one, and then write a résumé to apply for the job.

Reading/Language Arts Skills: writing—résumés • comprehension—following directions • spelling

Curricular Areas: social studies

Materials: newspaper help-wanted ads • (optional: sample copies of résumés)

Students will start thinking—"Who am I?" "What do I have to offer?"—as they put it all together in a résumé.

PREPARATION: Have students bring in the help-wanted section from newspapers.

DISCUSSION: What is a résumé? (a summary of a job applicant's previous job experience, education, and interests) How is it different from a job application? (A job application is a form and it asks for specific information; a résumé is written by the job applicant and contains more detailed information.) What are some important things you would want to put in your résumé? (name, address, education, volunteer and paid job experience, and so on)

DIRECTIONS:
1. Please look through the help-wanted section of the newspaper and read about the jobs that are available.
2. Choose a job you may be interested in doing someday.
3. Pretend you have the education and experience for the job. On paper list all of the reasons you would be qualified for the job. (education, experience, organization skills, personal interests, and so on)
4. Now, write a résumé in your best printing. Be sure to check your spelling. (Have students complete Activity Sheet 5-6.)

VARIATION: Have students create a résumé showing their qualifications for a job they can actually do now, such as house cleaning, baby-sitting, or yardwork.

Step to Success—Write a Résumé

Résumé

NAME: _____

ADDRESS: _____

_____

TELEPHONE: _____

EDUCATION:
(Include the name and city of each school attended. List the school most recently attended first.)

_____

_____

_____

WORK EXPERIENCE:
(List the job most recently held first. Include a brief explanation of your work responsibilities.)

_____

_____

_____

VOLUNTEER EXPERIENCE:
(Include school and community involvement.)

_____

_____

HOBBIES AND INTERESTS:

_____

_____

OTHER INFORMATION:
(Include any special awards you've received.)

_____

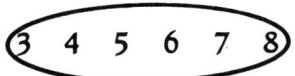
Classroom Chores— A Problem?

Students list the chores that need to be done to have a clean, organized classroom. Then they meet in small groups to determine how chores will be done, when, by whom.

Reading/Language Arts Skills: **critical thinking—comparing and contrasting • handwriting • writing—job descriptions**

Curricular Areas: **social studies • home economics • art**

Materials: **colored markers • tagboard • construction paper • scissors • stapler • class list**

Got a problem with classroom chores? Let the students take over and solve it!

DISCUSSION: Why would we want a clean, organized classroom? (easy to locate things, efficient, looks nice, and so on) Since this is our room, who should help take care of it?

DIRECTIONS:
1. Let's think about some chores that would help us have a better classroom. I will write them on the chalkboard as you brainstorm ideas. (pick up floor scraps, erase the chalkboard, straighten chairs, and so on)

2. Now let's look at the list. Do we need to do all these chores? Are there any that are the same as others? (Develop a list of chores that need to be done by crossing off and combining chores as students suggest.)

3. How should we select the helpers to do the chores? How often should helpers be changed to give others a chance to help? (Decide where to display the list of helpers.)

4. (Divide the class into three groups and assign each group one of the following tasks:)

    Group 1
    Using the class list, make a name card from tagboard for each student.

    Group 2
    Using the list of chores from the board, make a card from tagboard for each chore.

    Group 3
    Design and put up a bulletin board display. Cut out letters and designs to decorate the board.

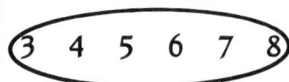

VARIATION: Have students write job descriptions for your classroom chores. A word processor would be useful for this chore.

Plan Ahead

Students make a weekly schedule that includes time slots for doing homework assignments, household chores, and recreational activities.

Reading/Language Arts Skills: **study skills—schedules • listening—following directions**

Curricular Areas: **mathematics • home economics • social studies**

Materials: **writing or graph paper for each student**

Ten minutes of planning a week on Monday morning can develop some valuable time-saving techniques for students and can result in long-lasting good work habits!

DISCUSSION: Have you ever wanted to do something really exciting but couldn't because you hadn't finished your chores or your homework? How many of you have forgotten all about a homework assignment or an important test until the last minute? What might help you to organize your time so that you aren't so likely to forget these important jobs?

DIRECTIONS:

1. Today you will make a schedule for the week. On your schedule, you will include time for chores and assignments that must be done, as well as time for those activities you do just for fun.

2. Divide your paper into five (or seven) columns. At the top of each column, write a day of the week. You may use abbreviations. (Use the chalkboard to demonstrate for students.)

3. On the left-hand side of the paper, just below the first day of the week, write the time you get up in the morning. Leave some space and then write the time you go to school. Just below that, write the time you get out of school. In the bottom left-hand corner, write the time you usually go to bed. List the hours that come between these times at even intervals down the left side of your paper.

4. Now, decide on a time each day when you can set aside an hour (30 minutes, two hours) to do homework. Write the word *homework* in each column across from the time slot you have chosen.

5. In the same way, fill in the chart with your daily or weekly chores. Are there any special activities going on (television shows, birthday parties, sports events) that you would like to fill in on your schedule? (Time for homework or chores may be adjusted to accommodate special activities.)

MON.	TUES.	WED.	THURS.	FRI.
6 a.m.				
7 a.m.				
8 a.m.				
3 p.m.				
4 p.m. Homework	Homework	Homework	Homework	Homework
5 p.m.				
6 p.m.				
7 p.m.				
8 p.m.				
9 p.m.				

6. (Repeat this activity each week. Your students should become expert time managers!)

VARIATION: If database software is available, have students develop a form that can be used to revise their schedules on a weekly basis.

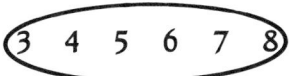
Quick and Easy

A. MAKING MAD MONEY

1. Make up sentences that describe ways to earn money. The words in each sentence should start with the same letter of the alphabet.

> Mary makes motorcycles.
> Doug digs ditches.

2. Write career-related sentences in which each word starts with consecutive letters of the alphabet.

> Maria notarizes old papers.
> Alan bakes cookies.
> Dennis entertains for general hospitals.

B. WHO WORKS HERE?

1. What jobs have to be done to run a hospital? Make a list of all of the different workers you can think of in a hospital.

2. (Repeat the activity for a different workplace: school, police station, airport, zoo, construction site, yo-yo factory, and so on.)

C. I'M THINKING OF A CAREER

1. (Think of a career. Give the class one clue at a time about what the career is: "This career requires four years of college." "This career requires that you work outdoors." After each clue, ask a student to try to guess what the career is. Keep giving clues until someone guesses correctly. Then have that person think of the next career.)

2. (Think of a career. Have students take turns asking yes or no questions about the career: "Do you work in an office?" "Does this career require that you travel?" Have students continue to ask questions until someone guesses the correct career.)

D. CREATIVE LICENSES

1. You are in charge of registering personalized license plates at the Department of Motor Vehicles. Decipher the five license plates you registered today. (Write the license plates on the chalkboard. The answers are in parentheses.)

> For a luxury car: 42N8 MAN (Fortunate man)
>
> For an athlete's car: 10S NE1 (Tennis anyone)
>
> For a station wagon: 7 GRT KDS (7 great kids)
>
> For a dentist's car: B DK FREE (Be decay free)
>
> For a florist's car: N2 FLWRS (Into flowers)

2. Invent your own personalized license plates. You can use up to eight characters; spaces don't count. See if your classmates can decipher your plates.

E. 101 USES

1. You are the manager of a grocery store. On the last order form, you accidentally ordered too many cotton-tipped swabs. When the shipment came, you received 10,000 boxes. In order to sell them quickly, you make a display showing all the uses you can think of for cotton-tipped swabs. Write as many uses as you can think of.

2. Do the activity with a different product (cotton balls, lemons, macaroni, toothbrushes, Ping-Pong balls, swimming goggles, pencils, chop sticks, and so on).

F. YOU'RE THE BOSS!

1. You're the boss. What traits do you look for when you are interviewing prospective employees? Make a list.

2. What characteristics do you like to see in a worker you have already hired?

G. JOB SEARCH

1. Imagine that you need a job. Make a list of ways you could go about looking for a job. (read the help-wanted ads, place an ad, post a notice on a community bulletin board, talk to friends and relatives, send a résumé)

2. Look at your list. Which do you think would be the most successful method of finding a job?

H. BABY SITTER'S IDEA KIT

1. Suppose you're baby-sitting two- and three-year-old children. Let's brainstorm all the things you could do to entertain them, and I'll write your answers on the chalkboard. Do not include watching television! (read storybooks, play ball, build blocks together, tell a story, draw a picture, and so on) Now, write the ideas down so that you'll be ready with your own baby-sitting idea kit!

2. (On another day, repeat this activity for baby-sitting different aged children.)

I. JOB SKILLS

1. (On the chalkboard, make a chart with six columns. Label them *reading, writing, handwriting, spelling, listening,* and *speaking.* Have students make the same chart on lined paper at their desks.)

2. What occupations require reading skills? (newscaster, actor, proofreader, journalist, letter carrier, secretary, and so on) List as many occupations as you can think of in the reading column. Do the same for the other language skills.

3. How many different occupations did you think of that require reading? What are they? (List student responses on the board.)

4. (Continue listing occupations that require the various language skills in the appropriate columns.)

Entertainment and Leisure Time

Sports Page Synonyms   Activity 6-2

1. *Comic Strip Punctuation*

2. *Sports Page Synonyms*

3. *The Guide Game*

4. *Good Sport Sporting Goods*

5. *Hobbies and Interests*

6. *Let It Snow!*

7. *Way to Go!*

8. *Quick and Easy*

    A. *Popular TV Shows*

    B. *My Very Own Computer*

    C. *Toying with Toys*

    D. *Spelling Words Go Up, Up, and Away*

    E. *Compounding the Fun*

    F. *For Your Viewing Pleasure*

    G. *25 Words or Less*

Welcome to the world of entertainment and leisure time. Sit back and enjoy yourself as you and your students discover entertaining and leisurely ways to reinforce reading and language arts skills.

Imagine what will happen when you tell your students that the latest television series, comic strip hero, or sporting event is going to help them learn! What kid could resist a chance to play "The Guide Game" or try "Comic Strip Punctuation" or look for "Sports Page Synonyms"? And what's more, your students will have a chance to apply their interests to real-life situations using maps, invoices, catalogs, and the television guide.

If your students are feeling especially creative, have them make up their own consumer games using the board and spinner on pages 277 and 276. Or they can pattern the games after ones they play at home, ones they see on television, or ones from this book. (See inside back cover for list of games.)

So relax and have fun! Use these activities to "turn on" student interest and "fine-tune" language skills!

Comic Strip Punctuation

Students practice correct use of capitalization, quotation marks, and other punctuation by rewriting comic strip captions as dialogue.

Reading/Language Arts Skills: **mechanics of writing—punctuation, capitalization • comprehension—sequence of events • writing—dialogue**

Curricular Areas: **art**

Materials: **Activity Sheets 6-1a and 6-1b (pages 161 and 162) or comic strips cut from newspapers (one for each student) • overhead projector and one transparency • (optional: correction fluid)**

Why not have Charlie Brown, Garfield, and Cathy help you to teach punctuation?

PREPARATION: Have students bring in comic strips from the daily newspaper. Comics that have dialogue between two or more characters work best for this activity. Make an overhead transparency of one strip to use as an example for the class.

DISCUSSION: How does a cartoonist show that the characters in a comic strip are talking to each other? (Their words are written in speech bubbles.) When we write a story, how do we show that the characters are speaking? (by using quotation marks)

DIRECTIONS:
1. Today we will practice using quotation marks and other punctuation by rewriting comic strips.
2. (Display the sample strip on the overhead projector.) Who is talking in the first frame? What are the words being spoken? How can these words be rewritten as dialogue? (Be sure speaker words are included, for example, "This is a great book," said Charlie Brown.) Where will quotation marks go? Where will commas go? (Choose a student to write the dialogue on the chalkboard as answers are elicited from other class members. Some strips use all capital letters. Have students use correct upper and lower case letters.)
3. (Continue with each frame of the comic strip until the entire dialogue has been written on the chalkboard.)
4. (Pass out a comic strip or Activity Sheet 6-1a and 6-1b to each student.) Please rewrite the comic strips as dialogue. When you have finished, pass your writing to a classmate and see whether he or she agrees with the way you have punctuated it.

VARIATIONS:

1. Use correction fluid to cover the words in the comic strip bubbles. Have students write their own words based on the events pictured in the strip.

2. As a sequencing activity, cut the comic strip frames apart and mix them up. Hand each student a set to put back into the proper order. If the comic strip has no speech bubbles, more than one sequence may be appropriate.

Comic Strip Punctuation

Rewrite each comic strip conversation. Be sure to use proper punctuation.

THE CONSUMER KIDS

_____

_____ said Eric.

_____ asked Stephanie.

_____ answered Eric.

THE CONSUMER KIDS

_____

_____ said Mr. Corley.

_____

_____ replied Ernie.

Comic Strip Punctuation

Rewrite each comic strip conversation. Be sure to use proper punctuation.

THE CONSUMER KIDS

_____ sighed Ralph.

_____ asked Gina.

_____ replied Ralph.

_____

_____ asked Gina.

THE CONSUMER KIDS

_____

_____ said Kate.

_____ exclaimed Jan.

Sports Page Synonyms

Students work alone or in groups to find verbs in newspaper sports articles and then make a chart listing common verbs and colorful synonyms for them, just as sportswriters do! (*See photo, page 157.*)

Reading/Language Arts Skills: **grammar and usage—verbs, adverbs, adjectives • vocabulary— synonyms • study skills—skimming**

Curricular Areas: **physical education**

Materials: **sports section of the newspaper for each student • notebook paper • scissors • stapler • colored pens**

Whether it's time for the Superbowl, the World Series, or the teachers' bowling tournament, it's the perfect time for this sports page activity.

DISCUSSION: How do sportswriters make an article about a baseball (bowling, volleyball, and so on) game exciting for their readers? How would the sports page sound if the writers used the same words over and over again?

DIRECTIONS: (You may wish to have students work in groups.)

1. We're going to look for different verbs used by sportswriters. What are some common verbs that describe the action during a game? (run, throw, kick, score, and so on) Let's list our responses on the board. What are some vivid verbs used to describe a team's performance in a game? (beat, trounced, edged, and so on)

2. Find an article in your sports section that describes a game. Skim the article and look for verbs. Circle all verbs with a colored pen. What are some of the verbs you found? Are these verbs synonyms for any of the common verbs we've listed?

3. We're going to make charts to show colorful verbs used in sportswriting. Please divide your paper into four (or eight) sections. Label each section with a common verb that might describe the action during a game. Then search the article for more exciting verbs used to describe the same actions. Write them on your chart in the proper sections. (Example: *run*— dash, blitz, charge) Cut out the article you used and staple it to your chart.

4. (After students have finished:) Let's share the charts. What are some of the interesting verbs you found? Are the same verbs used to describe different sports?

VARIATIONS:

1. Instead of verbs, have students skim sports articles to find adverbs and adjectives used to make a story more interesting.

2. Have students skim articles in other sections of the newspaper (travel, business, local news, food, science). Do these articles contain the type of verbs (adverbs, adjectives) found in a sports story?

3. Some students might like to listen to a game on the radio or watch one on television to find out what the sportscaster does to make the broadcast more interesting. (gives player statistics, tells anecdotes, and so on)

4. Have students look at a photo of a sports event or an athlete in action. Tell them to make a list of verbs that describe the action.

The Guide Game

Students use the television guide to find out what shows are on TV at a specified time on a certain day and how long they last.

Reading/Language Arts Skills: study skills—schedules

Curricular Areas: mathematics

Materials: **game board (page 277) • game spinner (page 276) • paper clips and pencils • playing piece for each student (coin, ring, or button) • television guide • tally sheet (notebook paper)**

Kids may discover that the television guide can be just as entertaining as the television!

PREPARATION: To make game board:

1. Duplicate a game board (page 277) for each group of students.

2. Students fill in each space on the game board, including the diamond and circle spaces, with a time of day written to the hour or half hour (9:00 p.m., 11:30 a.m., 3:30 p.m.). Times may be used more than once.

3. Students write POPULAR SHOW—RERUNS in the circle blanks and SHOW CANCELED in the diamond blanks.

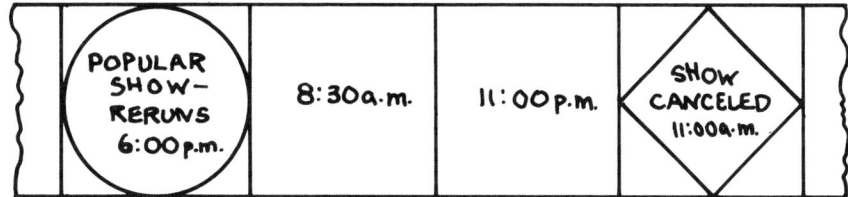

To make spinner:

1. Duplicate two game spinners (page 276) for each group of three or four students.

2. On one spinner, fill in each of the five sections with a different day of the week.

3. On the other spinner, fill in the five sections with the numbers 1,2,3,4,5.

To make players' tally sheets:

Tell students to fold a sheet of notebook paper in half lengthwise to make two columns. At the top of the left-hand column, have students write TELEVISION SHOW; at the top of the right-hand column, have them write LENGTH OF TIME, IN MINUTES.

DIRECTIONS:

1. Players spin the number spinner and the person with the highest number goes first. This person spins again and moves his or her piece the given number of spaces.

2. Players spins the day spinner. The player uses the television guide to find a show that starts at the time named on the space and the day named on the spinner. The player records the name of the show and its duration on the tally sheet.

3. If a player lands on a diamond space, no time is recorded on the tally sheet. If a player lands on a circle space, the length of time is doubled.

4. Play continues to the left. For each turn, the player spins a number, moves, spins a day, and then records the name of the show and its duration.

5. Play continues until all players reach the finish line. Players total the amount of television time they have accumulated. The winner is the player with the lowest total—the one who spent the least amount of time watching TV!

VARIATIONS:

1. The winner is the person who has the most television shows on his or her tally sheet.

2. For extra math practice, students choose a television show and calculate the ending time using information from the guide.

3. Have students keep a log of the shows they watch each day for an entire week. They can total the length of the programs to find the number of hours they spend watching television each week.

Good Sport Sporting Goods

Students fill out invoices for sports equipment.

Reading/Language Arts Skills: **study skills—invoices • comprehension—classifying • listening—following directions • handwriting**

Curricular Areas: **mathematics • physical education • art**

Materials: **sporting goods ad (page 169) • invoices (page 170) • (optional: sporting goods catalogs and newspaper ads)**

Exercise your students' imaginations as they select equipment for the ideal sports program.

PREPARATION: Make one copy of the sporting goods ad (page 169) and insert realistic prices for the items. Duplicate ads and invoices (page 170) for students.

DISCUSSION: Imagine that you are in charge of organizing an after-school sports program. Think about some of the sports you would like to offer in the program. What kinds of equipment would you have to buy for these activities?

What is an invoice? (statement of amount due) What information is on an invoice? (date, items purchased, quantity, cost per item or unit price, total price)

DIRECTIONS:
1. We'll use invoices to order the equipment needed for our sports program from Good Sport Sporting Goods. Let's do one invoice together. Let's say that we want to offer badminton in our sports program. We'll need a net. How much will that be? How much for two badminton racquets? How much for three shuttlecocks?

2. Please list these items and their prices on your first invoice. Be sure to include the quantity, the unit price, and the total price of each item.

3. Label the next three invoices A, B, and C. Follow these guidelines to choose the items for these invoices. (Write on the chalkboard or display on an overhead projector:)

   Invoice A:

   1 item to wear
   1 ball
   1 item to use with a ball
   1 other item

Invoice B:

1 of the most expensive item
1 of the least expensive item
2 baseball bats
2 tennis racquets
2 of any item of your choice

Invoice C:

Choose any items you wish for one particular sport. Write the name of the sport at the bottom of your invoice.

4. Write the items and their prices on your invoices. Be sure to print clearly.

VARIATIONS:

1. For a wider selection of items, use sporting goods catalogs or newspaper ads.

2. As a math activity, have students estimate the total for each invoice and then calculate the exact total.

3. Have students design a flier announcing their sports program. The flier could include a list of sports to be offered along with information about the location and the schedule for the program.

4. Have students use a computer graphics program to design their own invoices and fliers.

GOOD SPORT SPORTING GOODS

Baseball	$	.
Softball	$	.
Soccer ball	$	.
Volleyball	$	.
Tennis balls		
can of 3:	$	.
Ping-Pong balls		
box of 6:	$	.
Shuttlecocks		
can of 3:	$	.

Skateboard	$	.
Skates	$	.
Volleyball net	$	.
Tennis net	$	.
Badminton net	$	.

Tent	$	
Sleeping bag	$	.
Lantern	$	.

Baseball glove	$	.
Softball glove	$	.
Baseball bat	$	.
Baseball cap	$	.

Basketball	$	.
Backboard, goal,		
and net	$	.

Girl's bathing suit	$	.
Boy's swimming		
trunks	$	.
Running shoes	$	.
Sweat suit	$	.

Tennis racquet	$	.
Badminton racquet	$	.
Ping-Pong paddles		
2 for:	$	.

INVOICE NO. _____		DATE _____		
GOOD SPORT SPORTING GOODS				
923 FAIRPLAY COURT				
TEAMFIELD, CT 06802		Unit		Total
Qty.	Item	Price		Price
		Total		
		Cost		

INVOICE NO. _____		DATE _____		
GOOD SPORT SPORTING GOODS				
923 FAIRPLAY COURT				
TEAMFIELD, CT 06802		Unit		Total
Qty.	Item	Price		Price
		Total		
		Cost		

INVOICE NO. _____		DATE _____		
GOOD SPORT SPORTING GOODS				
923 FAIRPLAY COURT				
TEAMFIELD, CT 06802		Unit		Total
Qty.	Item	Price		Price
		Total		
		Cost		

INVOICE NO. _____		DATE _____		
GOOD SPORT SPORTING GOODS				
923 FAIRPLAY COURT				
TEAMFIELD, CT 06802		Unit		Total
Qty.	Item	Price		Price
		Total		
		Cost		

Hobbies and Interests

Students write short paragraphs explaining their favorite hobbies and then draw pictures showing themselves involved in their hobbies.

Reading/Language Arts Skills: **writing—descriptive paragraphs • grammar and usage—sentences • mechanics of writing—capitalization, punctuation • spelling • study skills—bar graphs • creative expression**

Curricular Areas: **art • social studies • mathematics**

Materials: **drawing paper • markers, crayons, or poster paints • thumb tacks or tape**

Here's a chance for all the students in your class to share something very special about themselves.

PREPARATION: Prepare an area on a large bulletin board or the chalkboard where pictures can be classified and arranged to build a giant bar graph.

DISCUSSION: How do you entertain yourself when you're on your own? What are your hobbies and other special interests (other than watching television)? (collections, models, games, toys, puzzles, building things, reading, sewing, writing, sports, cooking, drawing, gardening, and so on)

DIRECTIONS: 1. Think of yourself enjoying your favorite hobby or special interest. Write a short paragraph describing your hobby or special interest. Tell about the materials or equipment you use, and describe what you do. Be sure to use complete sentences and check for correct spelling, capitalization, and punctuation. Then draw a picture showing yourself involved in your hobby or interest.

2. (After pictures are finished:) What are some ways we could classify our hobbies and special interests? (sports, music, collections, arts and crafts, and so on) Let's sort the pictures into groups. (Write headings across the board.)

3. Please decide which heading best describes your hobby and put your picture on the board below it. (Have students start attaching their pictures along the bottom of the board under the best heading; when two or more pictures fall under the same heading, put one above the other to build a bar graph.)

Let It Snow!

Students use pictures from magazines and catalogs to make a mobile of a planned day in the snow.

Reading/Language Arts Skills: **comprehension—classifying • creative expression**

Curricular Areas: **art • social studies • physical education**

Materials: **winter issues of magazines and catalogs • construction paper • paste • scissors • string • single-hole punch**

Students find it hard to resist playing in the snow and will be eager to share their big plans as they practice consumer decision-making.

PREPARATION: Cut string into 20-inch lengths and give a length to each student.

DISCUSSION: Imagine you're planning a day or a vacation in an area that has lots of snow. What kinds of clothes will you need? Will you need special shoes or boots? What will you do in the snow? (ski, go sledding, build snow forts, and so on) What sporting equipment will you want to take along? What snacks can you bring for quick energy?

DIRECTIONS:

1. Look through the magazines and catalogs and cut out pictures of things you will need for your day in the snow. Draw pictures of any things you cannot find.

2. Paste the pictures onto construction paper. When you cut out the pictures, include some of the construction paper and cut out different shapes—circles, triangles, squares, and rectangles.

3. Lay the pictures out as you would like them on your mobile.

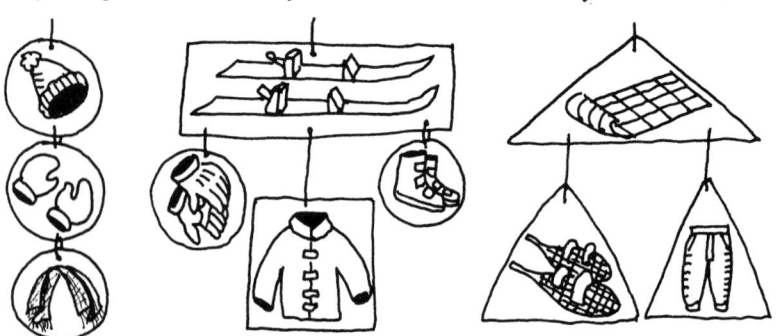

4. Punch a hole near the top or the bottom of each picture, depending on where it will connect to the other pictures.

5. Cut your string into pieces at least 3 inches long. Use them to connect your pictures to form a mobile.

6. When you are finished, you will share your mobile with the class by showing it and telling about your big plans in the snow!

Way to Go!

Students do a variety of activities using maps of their city, state, or country.

Reading/Language Arts Skills: study skills—maps • writing—directions, essays, critiques • handwriting • spelling • creative expression

Curricular Areas: social studies • mathematics

Materials: city map, page 175 • city, state, or country maps (one for each group of three or four students) • paper and pencils • (optional: graph paper)

Students are sure to have fun finding their way through this activity! And don't worry! Maps are easy to get from your chamber of commerce, real estate office, or automobile club. (See page 266.) Of course, you can always get one map and make copies for everyone.

PREPARATION: Make copies of the city map (page 175).

DISCUSSION: In what ways have you used maps? When have your parents used maps? Why are maps important?

DIRECTIONS: (Distribute maps and give students 10 or 15 minutes to look at them before starting any of these activities. Choose activities based on the maps you have available.)

BIKE IT!

(Provide the city map on page 175 or a map of your own city.) You just got a new bike and want to ride it in town, but your parents are afraid you'll get lost! Look at the map and choose where you want to go. Then write down the directions so you and your parents will know where you are going. Now "bike it!"

GONE FISHING

(Provide state maps.) Starting from your hometown, plan a fishing trip in another town for a three-day holiday weekend. You will be able to travel a maximum of 400 miles in one day. Explain where you will go to catch the most fish, the name of the fishing spot, towns where you will stop to eat or rest, and about how much time you will spend traveling and fishing.

SUMMER VACATION

(Provide maps of the country.) It's summer and you can choose anywhere in the country to go! Look at the map and choose someplace special. Now write an essay explaining why you want to go there, what you will do there, and places and points of interest you plan to visit on the way. Hint: Look for states or cities of special interest, as well as state parks, lakes, oceans, and mountains. Enjoy your trip!

WHAT'S IN A NAME?

(Provide the city map on page 175 or a map of your own city.) Look at your city map to discover the many different street names. If you could change any of the names, which ones would you change? What would you change them to and why? Be creative and update selected street names so that people will remember them. (Optional: On a piece of graph paper, duplicate part of the city map showing your newly named streets.)

VARIATIONS:

1. See *Kids Are Consumers, Too! Real-World Mathematics for Today's Classroom*, Activity 7-7, "Map-ematics Fun," page 185.

2. If you have a computer map skills program, encourage students to try it out and to evaluate it. Have them write a brief report indicating the main strengths of the program, any major weaknesses, and one change they would recommend.

City Map (Use for Activity 6-7)

Quick and Easy

A. POPULAR TV SHOWS

1. (This is played like "Twenty Questions.") I'm thinking of a popular TV show. Try to guess what it is by asking me questions that can be answered yes or no.

2. (The student who guesses the show gets to think of the next one.)

B. MY VERY OWN COMPUTER

1. Computers can be programmed to perform a variety of tasks. Help me make a list on the chalkboard of things computers can be programmed to do. (play video games; keep track of finances; dial telephones; set timing devices on such things as burglar alarms, microwave ovens, and televisions; address envelopes; and so on)

2. Imagine that you have your own computer. You are a genius at programming. What wonderful things would you program your computer to do? (Make a list of students' ideas on the chalkboard.)

C. TOYING WITH TOYS

1. What are some of the ways mechanical toys operate? (They use batteries, solar power, wind-up gears, electricity, and computer chips.)

2. Let's list on the chalkboard toys and games that don't need mechanical devices to make them work. (teddy bear, checkers, truck, jump rope, and so on)

3. If you could make the first toy (or game) on the chalkboard work mechanically, what would the toy be able to do? How about the next toy?

4. (On another day, have students compare and contrast toys from their grandparents' childhood with toys today. Ask students what changes have been made.)

D. SPELLING WORDS GO UP, UP, AND AWAY!

1. You have been chosen to take a flight in a hot-air balloon! Using as many of your class spelling words as possible, explain what you will see and what you will take with you!

2. (At another time, students can use their spelling words to write about a vacation or a visit to a far-off land, a trip in a time machine, or an experience resulting from winning a big contest.)

E. COMPOUNDING THE FUN

1. (Give each student a brochure or booklet such as a travel brochure, a television guide, or a comic book. See pages 271 and 272 for information on obtaining materials.) Please look at your brochure or booklet and write down as many compound words as you can find.

2. (Students can also look for rhyming words, adjectives, proper nouns, and so on.)

F. FOR YOUR VIEWING PLEASURE

1. (You'll need a television schedule for this activity.) Has anyone heard about a good television show that will be on this week? (Encourage students to include shows that are related to science, history, or other areas of academic interest.)

2. (List recommended shows on the chalkboard, along with the dates and times they will be aired.)

3. (After shows have aired, discuss them with students.) How many of you watched this show? Did it live up to your expectations? What did you learn from it? Would you recommend it to someone else?

4. (If this activity becomes a weekly event in your room, students are bound to pay more attention to the television shows they are viewing.)

G. 25 WORDS OR LESS

1. (Write the following on the chalkboard:)

WIN A TRIP FOR TWO TO HAWAII!

2. You are going to enter this contest. In 25 words or less, write why you should win this trip to Hawaii. The most clever, humorous, and creative entry will win!

3. (On another day, substitute a different prize. Ask students for suggestions or use one of the following: 10-speed bicycle, rock concert tickets, swimming pool, a shopping spree.)

Holidays and Special Occasions

Poet-Tree and Other Decorations   Activity 7-3;   Valentine Couplets   Activity 7-7B

1. *Greeting Cards—Say It with Style*
2. *Holiday Hang-Ups!*
3. *Poet-Tree and Other Decorations*
4. *Cut-Ups!*
5. *So It's Your Birthday!*
6. *A Holiday Feast*

7. *Quick and Easy*
   A. *New Year's Resolutions*
   B. *Valentine Couplets*
   C. *St. Patrick's Green All Over*
   D. *"Eggstra" Advice for Spring*
   E. *For Mom and Dad*
   F. *Be Patriotic—Vote!*
   G. *Healthy Halloween!*
   H. *Thanks!*
   I. *Make a List and Check It Twice!*
   J. *Crazy Mixed-Up Greetings*

C H A P T E R 7

In our fast-paced, modern society there is comfort in preserving the tradition of celebrating holidays and other special occasions. These are the times we can experience the fun, warmth, and care of family and friends.

In the real world of consumerism, children soon discover the cost of enjoying these special times. In this chapter we have developed many ideas for decorating, gift giving, sending messages, party planning, and even games to play—with little or no cost involved. Many curricular skills are interwoven throughout the chapter. So go on—celebrate! Your students will be learning and reinforcing valuable skills—just for the fun of it!

And if your class, the P.T.A., student council, or other worthy cause is looking for a way to raise money, take a look at Project 8-1, "Holiday Telegrams: A First-Class Business," on page 207.

Merry Consumer Awareness and Happy New Learning!

Greeting Cards— Say It with Style

Students analyze and create greeting cards. (For quick and easy thank-you cards, see Activity 7-7H, "Thanks," on page 201.)

Reading/Language Arts Skills: **creative expression • writing—greeting cards, invitations • handwriting • spelling • comprehension—following directions**

Curricular Areas: **art • social studies**

Materials: **directions for pop-up card (page 183) • blank greeting cards (pages 184-186) • colored construction paper or light tagboard • 8½ x 11 in. white paper • fine-line black markers • crayons or colored markers • scissors • glue • used greeting cards • brads • (optional: simple coloring books for pattern ideas)**

This activity is sure to encourage an attitude of thoughtfulness—at the same time it reinforces reading and writing skills!

DISCUSSION: (After distributing two or more used greeting cards to each student:) Let's take a few minutes to look at our cards. Which one do you like best? Why? What makes some cards better than others?

DIRECTIONS: 1. Today we're going to make greeting cards for special people in our school. Let's name the people who make our school a special place. (custodian, cafeteria workers, classroom aide, principal, gardener, and so on)

2. (Give each student a piece of white paper, a copy of the thank-you card on page 184, or a copy of the "For Someone with Class" card on page 186.) Each of you may make your own card to say thank you to one of these people.

(Choose one or more of the following activities for a variety of creative greeting cards.)

DRAW, SWAP, AND WRITE

(Have students choose a special occasion or holiday and create an illustration for it on a blank card. Then have each student exchange cards with a classmate and write an appropriate greeting or short poem inside.)

CREATIVE AND CRAZY CARDS

Try one of these ideas for an unusual card.

1. Shape Cards: Draw a picture or use a picture in a coloring book as a pattern to create a shape card. Trace around the basic shape, cut it out, and use it for your card.

2. Pop-Up Cards: (Give each student a copy of the directions on page 183.) Follow these directions carefully to make a card with a center that pops up when opened. (You may have to demonstrate the procedure for younger students.)

3. Movable Cards: Create cards with movable parts by using brads (for example, wheels on a car may be attached with brads so that they will turn).

INVITATIONS TO CELEBRATIONS

(Give each student a copy of the invitation on page 185, or have them design their own invitations. If students are designing their own invitations, have them create an appropriate design for the occasion on the outside. Inside, have them include information about the type of celebration, the date, time, and location, and who is giving the party. Use the ideas below to create seasonal invitations.)

1. Holiday Invitations: Choose a shape (heart, pumpkin, egg, and so on) that is appropriate to the occasion, and cut your card in that shape.

2. Graduation Invitations: Roll your invitation up to look like a diploma and tie it with a ribbon.

3. Postcard Invitations: Make a picture postcard with a picture on one side and the party information and mailing address on the other. (These can be hand delivered or sent through the mail.)

HOLIDAY TELEGRAMS

(See Project 8-1, "Holiday Telegrams: A First-Class Business," page 207.)

GRAPHIC GREETINGS

(Students can use a computer graphics program to design their own computer greetings.)

Directions for a Pop-Up Card
(Use for Activity 7-1)

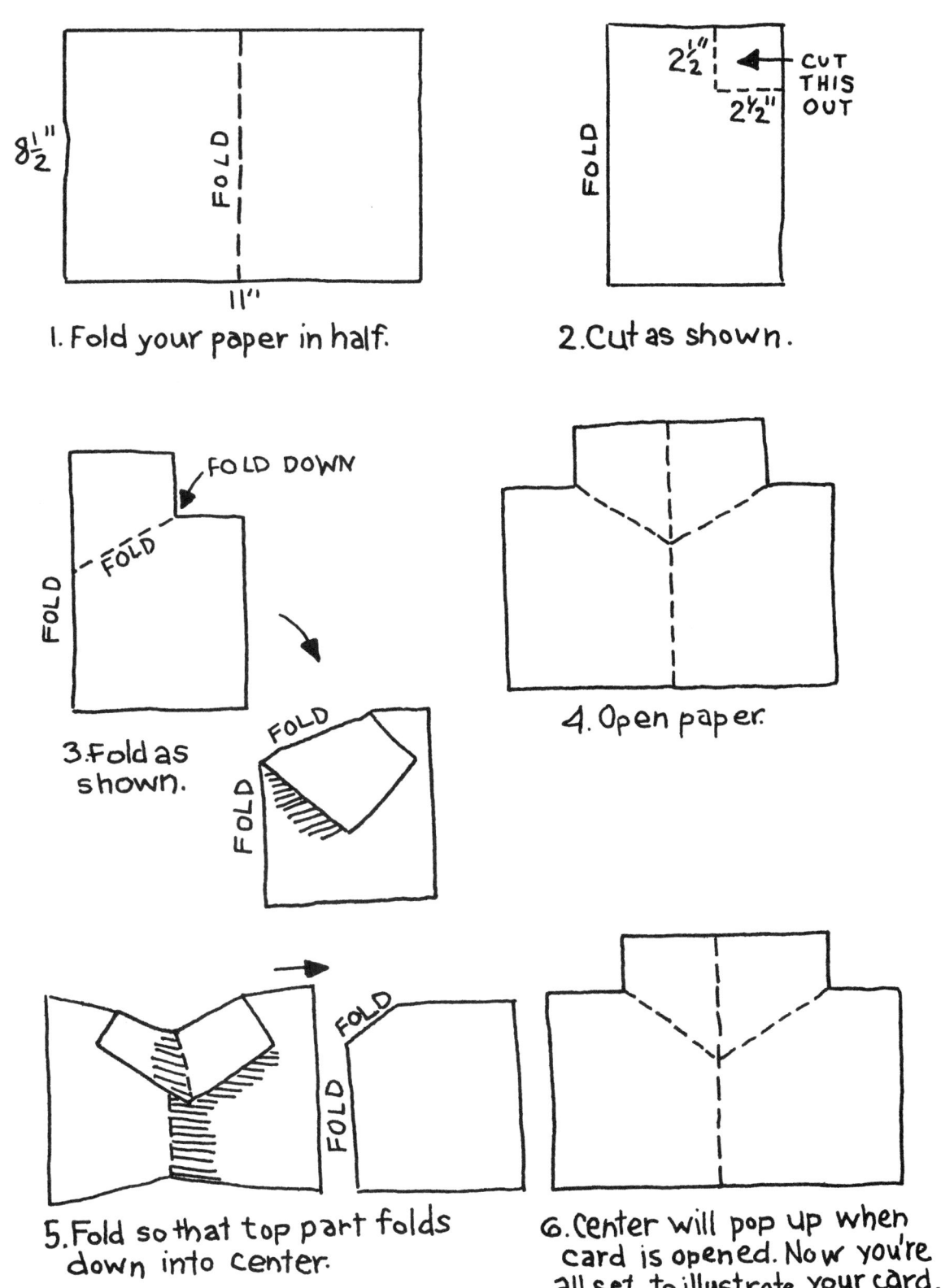

$8\frac{1}{2}$"

FOLD

11"

1. Fold your paper in half.

$2\frac{1}{2}$"

FOLD

$2\frac{1}{2}$"

CUT THIS OUT

2. Cut as shown.

FOLD DOWN

FOLD

FOLD

3. Fold as shown.

FOLD

FOLD

4. Open paper.

FOLD

FOLD

5. Fold so that top part folds down into center.

6. Center will pop up when card is opened. Now you're all set to illustrate your card.

Greeting Card (Use for Activity 7-1)

A "KIDS ARE CONSUMERS, TOO!" GREETING CARD

THANKS A BUNCH!

Chapter 7: Holidays and Special Occasions

Greeting Card (Use for Activity 7-1)

Hope you can attend!

_____

_____ Place:
_____ Time:
_____ Date:

_____
_____
_____ What?

A Special Event

A "KIDS ARE CONSUMERS, TOO!" GREETING CARD

Greeting Card (Use for Activity 7-1)

A "KIDS ARE CONSUMERS, TOO!" GREETING CARD

for Someone with Class

Holiday Hang-Ups!

Using a variety of art materials, students create wall hangings to express creative thoughts.

Reading/Language Arts Skills: creative expression • writing—phrases

Curricular Areas: art • social studies • science

Materials: felt tip markers • scissors • glue • metal clothes hangers • a large piece of construction paper or fabric scrap for each student • (optional: alphabet macaroni • glitter • lace, ruffles, and edging scraps • magazines and catalogs)

No matter what the occasion, you'll be proud to hang up these holiday banners.

DISCUSSION: What are some interesting things we could put on a wall hanging that would make it special? (holiday designs or greetings, funny sayings, photographs, and so on) What are some phrases we might want to use to express a special thought? (Suggest short lines from poems, songs, greeting card verses, proverbs and sayings, or phrases the students make up themselves.)

DIRECTIONS:
1. Take a piece of scrap paper and sketch a design for a wall hanging. Think about whom it is for, what type of message you want it to have, and what kind of picture or design you would like to make. With the materials provided, create your hanging. You can glue the top edges onto the bottom of a clothes hanger and let it dry so that it will be ready to hang.

2. (Students make wall hangings appropriate to seasonal holidays to display in class or at home.)

VARIATION: (Students create wall hangings that relate to units studied in class— for example, marine life, events in American history, or dinosaurs.)

Poet-Tree and Other Decorations

Students make "poem" bulletin boards, "adjective" wall designs, and "poetry" chains that are appropriate for a particular holiday, season, or special occasion. (*See photo, page 179*).

Reading/Language Arts Skills:	**writing—poems • grammar and usage—adjectives • creative expression • handwriting • spelling**
Curricular Areas:	**art • mathematics**
Materials:	**poem patterns (pages 191-192) • colored paper • drawing paper • crayons or markers • scissors • staplers • tape or glue**

When you show your students the "write" way to save money on holiday decorations—you'll be getting a holiday from your classroom decorating chores!

PREPARATION: Duplicate the poem patterns on appropriately colored paper.

DIRECTIONS: POET-TREE

1. (Design a bulletin board having a bare tree with lots of branches. Students may enjoy the chance to make the tree.)

2. Today we will be writing poems to go on our "Poet-Tree." The poems should be about autumn (upcoming holidays, birthdays, months, or seasons).

3. (Duplicate the leaf pattern on colored paper, using a variety of fall colors. Give each student a pattern.) Once you have finished writing your poem, rewrite it on the leaf pattern, cut it out, and staple it to the "Poet-Tree" bulletin board. (To tailor this activity to the other seasons, use these suggestions:)

   > Winter: (Students write poems on snowflake patterns. Arrange the snowflakes around the tree trunk and on the ground.)

   > Spring: (Copy the leaf and flower patterns on colored duplicating paper. Have students staple the leaves to the tree and the flowers to the ground.)

   > Summer: (Use the fruit pattern, or have students design their own patterns in the shapes of seasonal fruits. Have them staple the fruits to the tree.)

OUR "POET-TREE"

WALL DESIGNS AND BULLETIN BOARDS

1. (Distribute colored paper, scissors, glue, and other art supplies.)

2. Using a variety of shapes, make decorative designs or letters that spell out the name of the holiday or season for the bulletin board. Print an adjective on each shape to describe the holiday or season. (To tailor this activity to special occasions, use these suggestions:)

> Halloween: (pumpkins with eyes, noses, and mouths in the shape of triangles, squares, and circles. Possible adjectives: orange, spooky, haunted, eerie, scary.)
>
> Winter holiday: (snow sculpture and snow fort with snowball shapes, or pine tree with pine cone shapes. Possible adjectives: chilly, wet, happy, jolly, slushy, slippery, fragrant.)
>
> Spring: (plants with leaf and flower shapes. Possible adjectives: fresh, green, clean, fragrant, warm, cheerful.)
>
> School carnival: (balloon shapes decorating a scene depicting carnival booths and activities. Possible adjectives: fun, noisy, exciting, profitable.)

POETRY CHAINS

1. (Have students cut strips of colored paper to make chains.)

2. Make up the first line of a poem about this holiday (season, special occasion).

3. Print each word of your line of poetry on a separate paper strip. Put the strips together to form a chain.

4. Give your poetry chain to a friend. Your friend will read your line of poetry and add more links to form the next line which he or she will make up to go with yours.

5. (If time permits, have students start another poetry chain to pass on to another friend.)

6. (Optional) Choose at least two colors when making your poetry chain and create a color pattern. Your friend will need to continue the same color pattern as well as continue the poem. (For example, autumn: brown, gold, green, gold, orange, gold, brown, gold, green, gold, ... Valentine's Day: red, red, white, red, red, white, ... St. Patrick's Day: light green, dark green, light green, dark green, ... Patriotic holiday: red, white, and blue, ...

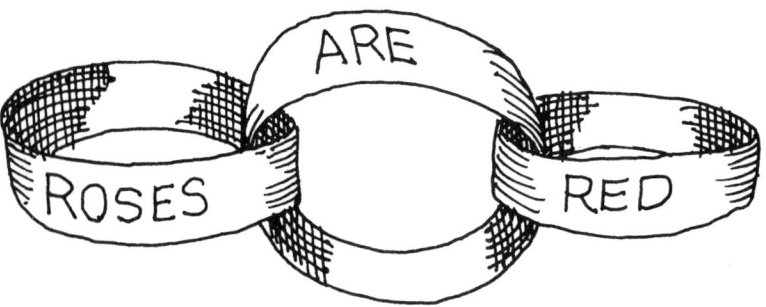

VARIATION: Have students make paper chain decorations as a way of keeping track of the books they have read. As students finish reading a book, have them write the book title and author and their own name on a strip of paper. Each strip can be added as a link on a class chain. As the chain grows, so will students' enthusiasm for reading!

Poem Patterns (Use for Activity 7-3)

Fall Leaf Pattern

Winter Snowflake Pattern

Poem Patterns (Use for Activity 7-3)

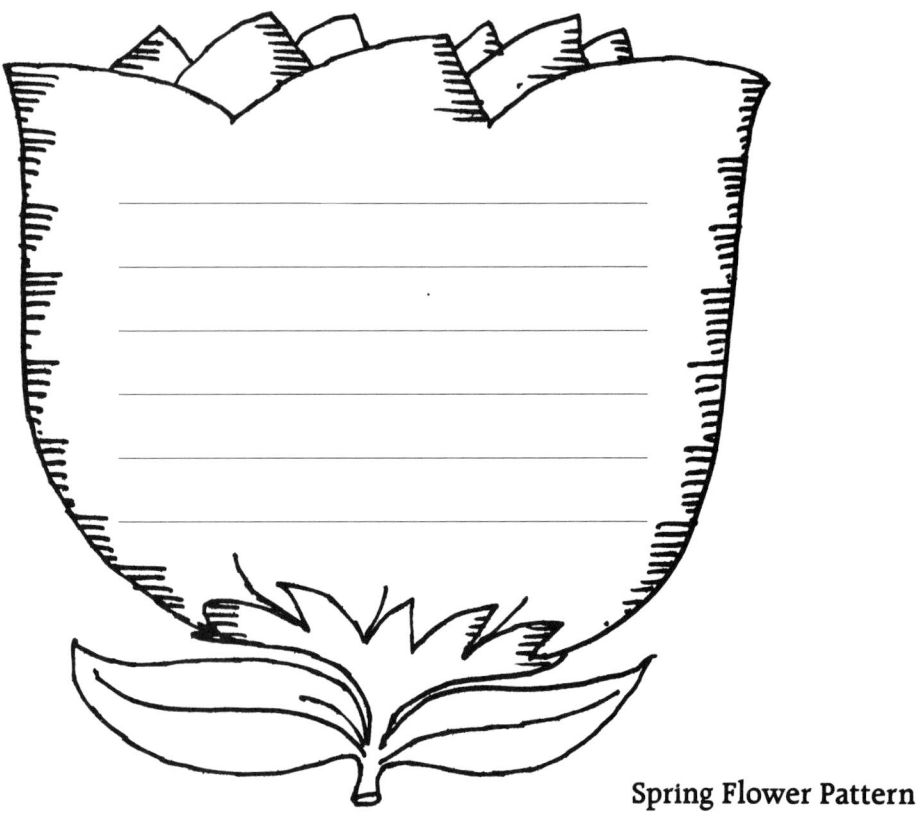

Spring Flower Pattern

Summer Fruit Pattern

Chapter 7: Holidays and Special Occasions

Cut-Ups!

Using magazines, students find action verbs that relate to a holiday. They cut out the verbs and put them in a container; then they take turns drawing a verb, acting it out, and asking the class to guess the verb.

Reading/Language Arts Skills: **grammar and usage—verbs • nonverbal communication**

Curricular Areas: **physical education**

Materials: **magazines • crayons or markers • scissors • coffee can or other container**

Do this activity and you'll have a container full of quick and easy fun for those spare moments in class!

DISCUSSION: What is an action verb? (a word that names an action) Can you give an example of an action verb? (laugh, think, run, talk, hop) Let's think of some action verbs that describe holiday activities. (sing, eat, bake, decorate, carve, dance, and so on)

DIRECTIONS:
1. Look through your magazines and find action verbs that could relate to a holiday. Circle them with a marker or crayon and cut them out. To make them easier to handle, cut out a larger section of the paper around each verb.

2. (Put the verbs in a container.) Who wants to go first? Come and draw a verb from the container without looking and then act it out.

3. Who can guess the verb? (Students take turns drawing a verb from the container, acting it out, and asking the class to guess the verb.)

4. (Keep the container on hand for a Quick and Easy activity.)

So It's Your Birthday!

From traditional greetings and gifts to a class "un-birthday" party, this activity provides a variety of ideas for celebrating birthdays.

Reading/Language Arts Skills: **writing—greeting cards, descriptive paragraphs • creative expression • handwriting • spelling**

Curricular Areas: **social studies • art • mathematics • home economics**

Materials: **birthday card (page 197) • gift certificate (page 107) • birthday booklet page (page 198) • white and colored paper • manila paper • tagboard • colored markers • recipe and ingredients for pretzels (page 27)**

Put away your birthday crown and pin-the-tail-on-the-donkey game, and get ready for a bright new batch of birthday ideas!

DIRECTIONS: (Choose one or more of the following activities for a student birthday celebration.)

BIRTHDAY CARD

1. (Give each student a copy of the birthday card on page 197. As an alternative, use the Gift-Gram on page 212.)

2. Write a birthday greeting for (name of student whose birthday is next) on the card.

BIRTHDAY GIFT CERTIFICATE

1. (See "Pick a Present for a Pal," Activity 4-2, for the gift certificate form on page 107. Duplicate one for each student.)

2. Think of something you could give to or do for (name of student whose birthday is next). (Let him or her be first in line to recess, be team captain, help grade papers, and so on.) Fill it in on the gift certificate form.

"YOU'RE SPECIAL" BOOKLET

1. (Give each student a copy of the birthday booklet page on page 198.) On the top half of the booklet page, draw a picture that shows something special about (name of student whose birthday is next). (smiles a lot, likes to ride horses, is a good basketball player, and so on) On the bottom half of the page, write a short paragraph about the person.

2. (Collect the drawings and make them into a booklet. On the front cover print "You're Special" and the student's name.)

BIRTHDAY AUTOGRAPHS

1. (With a sheet of tagboard and colored markers, have each student write a one-sentence message and sign his or her name. Sentences written in all directions make an interesting and attractive design to hang on the wall for special birthday memories.)

2. (Optional: Cut the tagboard into the shape of a cake, a candle, a favorite pet, or other appropriate shape before students write their messages.)

A BIRTHDAY GRAPH

(Have students prepare a class birthday graph showing whose birthdays fall in each month. See *Kids Are Consumers, Too! Real-World Mathematics for Today's Classroom*, "A Quick Birthday Graph," page 19.)

UN-BIRTHDAY PARTY

1. (Celebrate students' summer birthdays or have a class "un-birthday" party by making party pretzels! See Activity 1-8, "A Twisted Memory Teaser," page 25, for a pretzel recipe.)

2. Since this is your special "un-birthday," you may form the pretzel dough into any shape you like—your initials, your age in Roman numerals, your favorite animal, a hobby, and so on.

3. (For additional ideas, see *Kids Are Consumers, Too! Real-World Mathematics for Today's Classroom*, Project 8-1, "A Class Party," page 195.)

Birthday Card (Use for Activity 7-5)

A "KIDS ARE CONSUMERS, TOO!" GREETING CARD

HAPPY BIRTHDAY

Birthday Booklet Page (Use for Activity 7-5)

FOR A SPECIAL
PERSON ON A SPECIAL DAY

_____

_____

_____

_____

_____

_____

_____

_____

_____

_____

_____

A Holiday Feast

Students plan a special holiday meal and then collect food ads and discount coupons to find the best deals on the foods they've chosen.

Reading/Language Arts Skills: **critical thinking—comparing and contrasting, expressing opinions**

Curricular Areas: **home economics • mathematics • health**

Materials: **food ads and discount coupons from magazines, newspapers, and the mail • scissors • paste • drawing paper**

You can't eat a newspaper, but you can feast your eyes on the food ads!

PREPARATION: Ask students to bring in a variety of food ads and discount coupons from newspapers, magazines, and the mail.

DISCUSSION: Do you think people spend more or less money on food during the holidays than they normally do? (more) Why might a store or a manufacturer offer a discount on certain food items during this time? (to attract a large number of customers) Today we will search the ads for bargains to plan a special holiday meal.

DIRECTIONS: 1. Make a list of foods that you would like to serve for your meal. What food groups should you include? (vegetables, meats, dairy products, and grains) Don't forget to plan a dessert!

2. Now look through your food ads and see whether you can find any of the items on your list at discount prices. Look through the ads from different stores to find the one that offers the best buy. Can you find coupons for any of the items on your list?

3. On your drawing paper, neatly print a menu for your meal. Then paste the food ads and coupons for menu items on the paper.

4. (Once the papers have been completed:) Let's share our menus. Who found a real bargain on an item? Who found a discount coupon that really helped save some money? Was there a difference in price from store to store?

VARIATIONS: 1. As a math activity, have students calculate the total cost for the planned meal.

2. Students can use database software to create a file in which to store price information for various food items for a month. At the end of the month, they can compare prices and discuss the advantages and disadvantages of shopping with coupons.

Quick and Easy

A. NEW YEAR'S RESOLUTIONS

1. Pick a character from a familiar story or a book you have read. Write a list of New Year's resolutions that this person might make. (As a variation, students can write resolutions for a famous person in history or a prominent person in the news.)

2. (To help students set their own goals for the year, have them write their own personal lists of resolutions. Remind students to be realistic and set attainable goals.)

B. VALENTINE COUPLETS

1. Think of a line of poetry appropriate for Valentine's Day. Write it on a strip of paper. Remember, Valentine thoughts can be romantic, friendly, or funny! (Collect the sentences.)

2. (On another day, divide the class into two teams. Have a person from team A choose one of the lines of poetry without looking, and read it. Team B has two minutes to think of a rhyming sentence to form a couplet.)

C. ST. PATRICK'S GREEN ALL OVER!

1. (On the chalkboard make a chart with the following categories: food, beverages, plants, clothes, furniture. Students make the same chart on lined paper at their desks.)

2. Please look at the categories on your paper. Write down as many items as you can think of in each category that could be green. Use your imagination, as any bright leprechaun would surely do!

3. (On another day, change the categories.)

D. "EGGSTRA" ADVICE FOR SPRING

1. Springtime means hens are laying eggs by the dozens! Let's think of all the things we could do with eggs.

2. (Divide the class into four groups. Assign each group a different category of possible uses for eggs: crafts, food, games, gifts, and so on.)

3. Be creative and think of the things you could do with eggs in your group's category. Write them on a piece of paper.

4. Now let's hear all that "eggstra" advice! Which group wants to read its list first?

E. FOR MOM AND DAD

1. (For Mother's Day) Using the letters in the word *MOTHER*, make a list of things you could do for your mom as a Mother's Day present. (*M*ake dinner, *O*pen doors, *T*ake out the trash, *H*ug her, *E*mpty the dishwasher, *R*ake the lawn)

2. (For Father's Day, repeat the activity using the letters in the word *FATHER*.)

F. BE PATRIOTIC—VOTE!

1. Imagine that you are going to run for a public office as leader of your community, county, or country. Think of the traits that would make you a good candidate, and list them on a piece of paper. Which traits do you think would be most important for a public leader to have?

2. (If time allows, give each student a large piece of drawing paper. Ask them to design a poster that will make people want to vote for them. Place posters around the room and have the class discuss which characteristics are most important for public leaders to have.)

G. HEALTHY HALLOWEEN!

You are buying Halloween goodies for trick-or-treaters. Make a list of healthy treats. (small boxes of raisins; packages of sunflower seeds, nuts, or trail mix; individual cartons of juice; miniature bars of soap; children's toothbrushes; and so on)

H. THANKS!

1. (Pass out index cards or paper to each student.) Please write a quick thank-you poem or note to someone at school, at home, or in the neighborhood or community. Decorate the card if you like.

2. (On another day, do Quick and Easy Activity 2-10I, "The Mail Must Go Through," page 71.)

I. MAKE A LIST AND CHECK IT TWICE!

1. Make a list . . .
of things you'd like to do during vacation, presents you'd like to receive, people you'd like to visit, holiday food you want to eat, and so on.

2. And check it twice . . .
   by rearranging your list and putting the items in order from
   most to least important or from most to least expensive.

J. CRAZY MIXED-UP GREETINGS

1. (Cut used greeting cards in half, separating the cover from
   the inside. Put the cover greetings in one box and the inside
   messages in another box. Select two students to come before
   the class. Have one student, without looking, choose a cover
   greeting, show it to the class, and then read any greeting that
   is on it. Have another student, in like manner, choose and
   read an inside message. NOTE: The results can be quite
   interesting—and funny!)

2. (For another idea using used greeting cards, see Quick and
   Easy Activity 2-10C, "A Chalkboard Collage of Feelings,"
   page 69.)

Part 3.
Projects

Projects

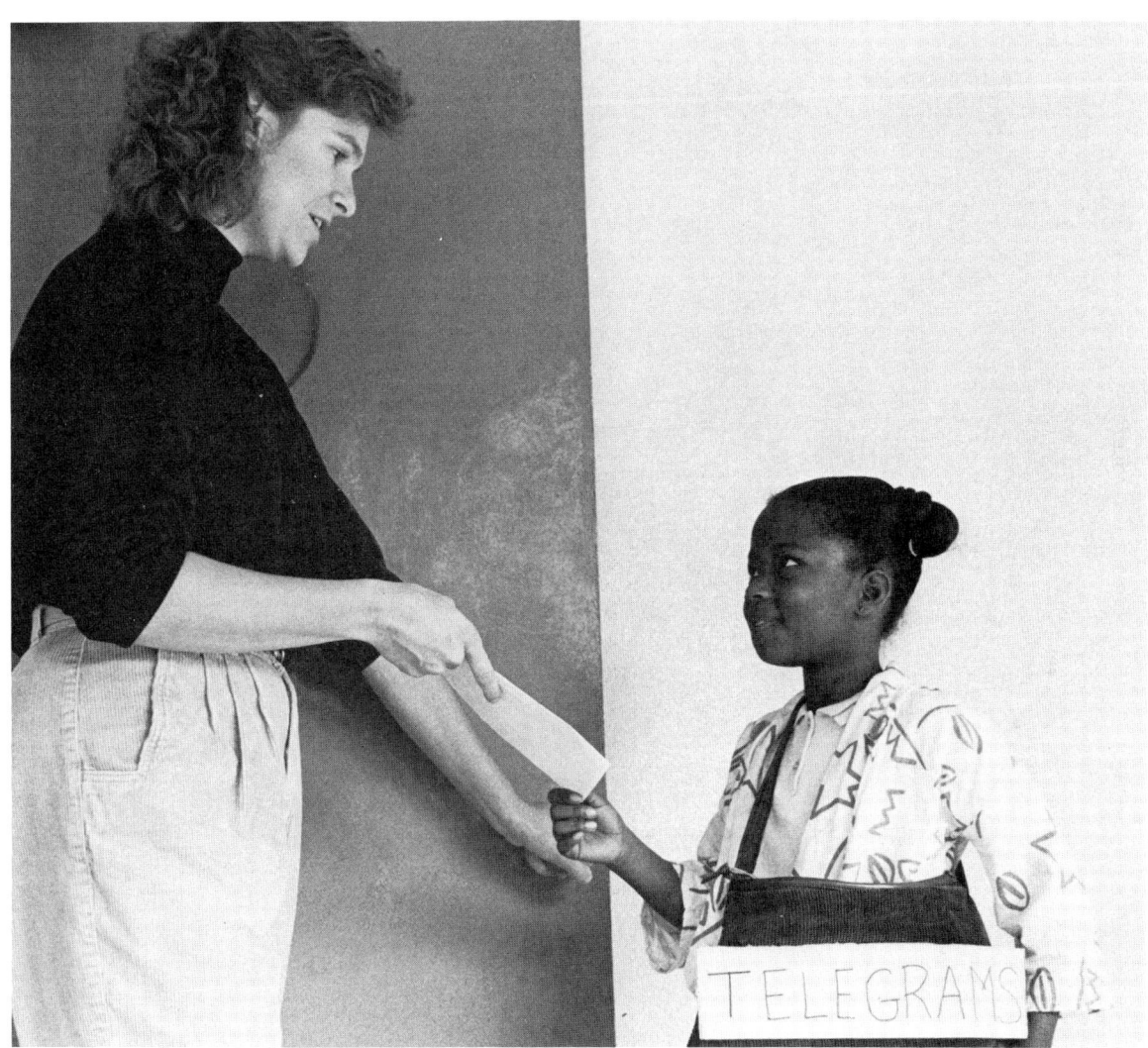

Holiday Telegrams: A First-Class Business   Project 8-1

1. *Holiday Telegrams: A First-Class Business*
2. *Let's Advertise Nationwide*
3. *Meet the Press: Getting to Know the Newspaper*
4. *Let's Form a Job Club*
5. *Career Day*
6. *Progress Report: A Straight-A School*

Here are six comprehensive class projects. Each offers an opportunity for your students to participate in real-world consumer experiences. And each provides a chance for every child to participate in cooperative learning and problem solving.

These projects require several days to several weeks to carry out (although most can be modified and shortened for one-day class use). We found that when our students spent this extended time on projects, they had a learning experience not otherwise possible. They gained in-depth practice with skills and concepts and gained a deeper understanding of consumer decision-making. In addition, students gained a sense of responsibility, pride, and confidence as they became involved in successful activities that brought the school and community closer together.

Although the emphasis is on reading and language arts, these projects are easily integrated with other curricular areas. When time runs short during reading and writing periods, you'll find these projects overlap nicely with social studies, math, and art. We hope this gives you the time you need—and gives your students the time of their lives!

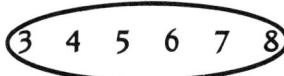

Holiday Telegrams: A First-Class Business

As a class project, students design and sell holiday telegrams to students and members of the school staff. Once messages have been written on the telegrams, class members deliver them anywhere in the school! (*See photo, page 205.*)

Reading/Language Arts Skills: **writing—telegrams, advertisements, business fliers • creative expression • handwriting • speaking—giving information • study skills—schedules • drama—role playing**

Curricular Areas: **mathematics • art • social studies**

Materials: **copies of selected telegram designs (pages 211-212) or student-designed telegrams • duplicator paper (optional: various colors) • poster paper • markers or crayons • pencils • cash box • telegram return box • (optional: calculators)**

This real-world activity "legalizes" note-passing while involving students in running a business of their own.

PREPARATION:

1. Discuss the idea of selling telegrams with your school principal to be sure the plan will be supported. If your principal or you prefer not to have students sell the telegrams, the project could be done as a class gift to the school.

2. The directions for the telegram sale are presented in three parts: (1) planning for the sale, (2) operating the sale, and (3) delivering the telegrams. It's important to start planning activities at least two weeks before the telegrams are to go on sale to allow enough time for designing the telegrams and advertising, as well as to be sure students know the necessary operating procedures.

DIRECTIONS:

PLANNING FOR THE SALE:

1. Selecting Telegram Designs

(Choose a telegram design (pages 211-212) appropriate to the time of the year, or have students design their own telegram forms. You may have students who would enjoy the challenge of using a computer graphics program to create their own telegram designs.)

2. Determining How Many Telegrams to Print

(Students should determine how many blank telegrams are needed to begin the telegram sale. They should consider the following questions:)

A. How many students are in our school?

B. What proportion of them will probably buy telegrams?

C. How many telegrams will each prospective customer probably buy?

3. Deciding on a Selling Price

(Allow students to determine a selling price for the telegrams. In order to ensure sales, it is best to keep the price relatively low. Have students keep in mind, however, the cost of duplicating the telegrams and the cost of the paper.)

4. Determining Sale Dates

(If you are doing this as a holiday activity, plan on selling telegrams for about one week, ending at least one day before that holiday. This will give your class a day for sorting the telegrams and scheduling delivery times.)

5. Choosing a Location for the Sale

(As students suggest various locations for the sale, have them discuss the pros and cons of each location. Help them understand the importance of a central location that will attract the largest number of students.)

6. Managing the Sale

(Have students identify management decisions that must be made before the sale starts. Some decisions to consider are:)

A. How long should telegrams be on sale?

B. How many salespersons are needed each time telegrams are being sold?

C. Who will be responsible for bookkeeping?

D. Who will be responsible for seeing that blank telegrams are duplicated as needed?

E. Where will the telegrams be stored?

7. Assigning Jobs

(Have students decide what types of positions will need to be filled: salespeople, bookkeepers, advertising experts, telegram printers, sorters, delivery people. A personnel committee can be responsible for hiring enough workers for each position. Each group of workers should determine how they will share responsibility for their job. Appointing a supervisor for each group may help students keep track of who is doing what job and when.)

8. Advertising the Sale

(Have students plan an advertising campaign to inform the school of the telegram sale. They can design posters and fliers or write announcements to be made over the school's intercom system or printed in the school newsletter.)

9. Training the Salespersons

(Have students role play what a salesperson does. Help them go through the following procedure for each purchase:)

A. Serve one customer at a time.

B. Count out the correct number of telegrams.

C. Calculate the total price.

D. Collect the money.

E. Count out the correct change.

F. Record the number of telegrams sold and the money earned.

10. Setting Up the Sale

(Have a committee plan the arrangement of furniture for the store. The basic items should include a table, a cash box, telegram forms, pencils, a telegram return box, and a display of the types of telegrams. The telegram display should include the following directions for the telegram purchasers:)

A. Write a message on the telegram form.

B. Fold the telegram in half and write the name and room number of the person who is to receive it.

C. Put the telegram in the telegram return box to be delivered.

OPERATING THE SALE:

1. The Grand Opening

(If the advertising campaign has been successful, you may have a huge crowd of customers the first day. To avoid overcrowding, designate certain times for each grade level to buy telegrams. Be sure to schedule a time for your class to purchase telegrams. You may wish to set aside a class period for telegram writing.)

2. Job Assignments

(A Sales Committee can take responsibility for assigning salespersons for each time period that the store is open. They should prepare a schedule for the week in advance and post it in a conspicuous place so that all students will be aware of the times they are scheduled to work.)

3. Bookkeeping

(A Bookkeeping Committee can be appointed to keep track of the telegrams sold and the money earned. Having the same students do this job regularly generally provides more accurate records than if it is done by different salespersons each day.)

DELIVERING THE TELEGRAMS:

1. Setting Up Delivery Times

(Before delivering the telegrams, have a student go to each classroom and schedule a convenient delivery time with each teacher. Since this project is suggested as a holiday activity, teachers may want to have telegrams delivered during class parties.)

2. Sorting Telegrams

(Assign a sorting committee to sort all telegrams by room number and delivery time.)

3. Delivering Telegrams

(Assign students to deliver the telegrams to classes at the scheduled times. Post the delivery schedule and the names of students responsible for delivery in a conspicuous place so that telegrams will be delivered at the proper times. If a student who is to receive a telegram is absent, the telegram can be delivered to that student's teacher or be delivered the next day.)

VARIATION: Offer singing telegrams or telegrams to be read aloud for a slightly higher price.

VALEGRAM

LEPRECHAUN
LETTER

GIFT-GRAM

GHOST-GRAM

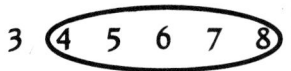
Let's Advertise Nationwide

Students create a product and then plan an advertising campaign to introduce it on a nationwide basis.

Reading/Language Arts Skills:	**creative expression • writing—product labels, commercials, advertisements, news reports • handwriting • speaking—doing commercials, interviewing**
Curricular Areas:	**social studies • art**
Materials:	**Task Cards 1-9 (pages 215-218) • white and colored paper • newsprint • tagboard • fabric scraps • old magazines • markers • glue or staplers • scissors • (optional: video camera and tape, VCR, television • tape recorder and cassette)**

Let this new and improved project take your students' imaginations all the way from the drawing board to the showroom floor.

PREPARATION: Duplicate one set of task cards for each small group of students.

DIRECTIONS:
1. (Divide the class into small groups. Give each group a complete set of task cards.)
2. Please read Task Card 1. Discuss it within your group and then follow the directions.
3. (After students have completed Task Card 1, have each group discuss and complete Task Cards 2 through 9.)
4. (Optional: As a grand finale to this project, invite parents and members of the business community to your class. Have students explain and share the results of their advertising projects.)

VARIATION: Whole Class Project
1. Describe the project to the class. Complete Task Card 1 as a whole group. (You may wish to refer to Activity 5-2, "Patent Pending," page 134, for ideas on creating new products.)
2. List the titles of the Task Cards on the board. Have students sign up for one or two tasks.
3. Plan a regular time each day to work on the advertising campaign.

Create a Product

(Use with Project 8-2.)

You are an inventor or designer. You're working on an exciting new product that will be sold in stores all across the country!

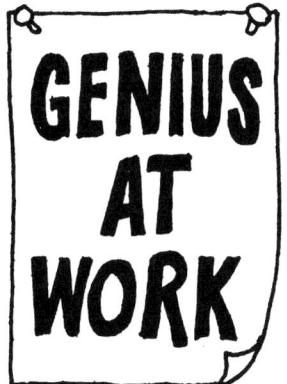

1. Create this new product. Decide the following things:
   A. What will the product do?
   B. How will the product work?
   C. What will the product look like?
   D. What will the product be called?
   E. Who will buy it?
   F. What kind of stores will sell the product?
2. Write a description of your product. Then draw a picture or diagram of the product, or make a model of it.

T	A	S	K	C	A	R	D	2

Design a Package

(Use with Project 8-2.)

You are a commercial artist at Creative Label and Box Company.

Materials You Will Need: colored paper • newsprint • tagboard • old magazines • markers • glue or a stapler • scissors

Design a package or a label for your new product. Remember that the label or package must meet three requirements:

1. It must be the right size and shape for the product.
2. It must tell important things about the product.
3. It must make people want to buy the product.

The Sales Representative

(Use with Project 8-2.)

You are a sales representative for the company that makes the new product. Your job is to persuade store owners that they should buy the product to sell in their stores.

1. Outline a phone call to a store manager. Remember the following things:
   A. This is the first time the manager has ever heard of the product.
   B. You want to arrange a meeting to demonstrate the product to the manager.
   C. You hope to be able to sell a lot of the product to the store.
2. Outline a demonstration to present at your meeting with the store manager.

Window Display

(Use with Project 8-2.)

You are the manager of a store that has decided to sell the new product.

Plan three window displays for the product:

1. Plan a display for the first day the product is available in your store.
2. Plan a display that will begin on December 10.
3. Plan a display for a sale several months later when you want to get the product off the shelves to make room for some new items.

A TV Commercial

(Use with Project 8-2.)

You are a producer of television commercials.

Plan and produce a TV commercial to advertise the new product on nationwide TV during a prime-time broadcast. (If video equipment is available, you may want to video tape the commercial and play it for the class.)

Things to think about:

1. People of all ages will see the commercial.
2. People in all parts of the country will see the commercial.
3. People must be convinced that they need or want the product.
4. People need to remember the name of the product or a catchy phrase about it.
5. People need to know where they can buy the product.

A Radio Commercial

(Use with Project 8-2.)

You are a producer of radio commercials.

Plan and produce a commercial to advertise the new product on one of the following radio stations:

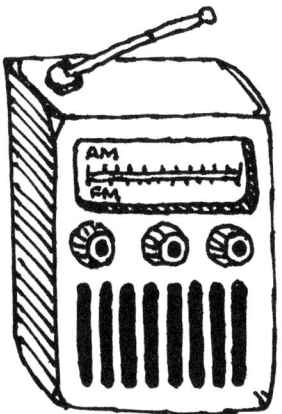

1. KPOP—a station that plays popular music all day
2. KNWS—a station that broadcasts only news, weather, and sports
3. WTLK—a station that broadcasts talk shows, discussions, and plays

(You may want to record the commercial on a tape recorder and play it for the class.)

Newspaper Ads

(Use with Project 8-2.)

You are the advertising manager of a large store that has decided to sell the new product. Your store will start selling the product next month. Design three half-page ads for the local newspaper:

1. One ad will run two days before the product goes on sale.
2. One ad will run the day the product is first available.
3. One ad will run two weeks later.

Magazine Ads

(Use with Project 8-2.)

You are a commercial artist for your favorite magazine.

1. Decide which magazine you work for.
2. Design a one-page ad for the new product that will appeal to the people who read the magazine.

Roving Reporter

(Use with Project 8-2.)

You are a reporter working for the local newspaper or TV station. The new product has been on the market for a month.

1. Interview your classmates to find out what they think of the new product. Be sure to plan your questions beforehand.
2. Prepare a report. You may either produce a TV news report or write a newspaper article about the new product.

Meet the Press: Getting to Know the Newspaper

Students become familiar with the newspaper through a variety of real-life language arts activities.

Reading/Language Arts Skills: **comprehension—comparing and contrasting, classifying • study skills—newspapers, skimming, classified ads • vocabulary—abbreviations, content area words, synonyms • critical thinking—expressing opinions • writing—summaries, advertisements • grammar and usage—verbs**

Curricular Areas: **social studies**

Materials: **newspapers (at least one per student) • Activity Sheet 1-7 (page 23) and Activity Sheet 8-3 (page 221) • scissors • glue • poster paper**

Need a reading text that motivates and challenges students, contains interesting and up-to-date information, and helps students practice a variety of reading skills? You'll find it right at your front door—the newspaper!

PREPARATION: Ask students to bring old newspapers from home (see sample letter to family, page 251). For other ways to get newspapers, see the suggestions on page 266.

DIRECTIONS: FRONT PAGE NEWS: Comprehension; study skills

(Familiarize students with the layout of the front page of the newspaper.)

1. The Banner

   Locate the banner. This is the name of the newspaper printed across the top of the front page. What is the name of your newspaper? How many pages does it contain? What is the date?

2. The Lead Story

   Find the lead story. It is usually located in the upper right-hand column. What is the lead story's headline? The second most important story is often found in the top left-hand column. What is its headline?

3. The Index

   You can usually find the newspaper index in a lower corner of the front page. What are some of the index headings? How are the headings arranged? What information would you find in the *weather* section? What information would you find in the *sports* section? Use the index to locate the classified ads.

4. The Columns

Information on a newspaper page is arranged in columns. How many columns are on the front page? Columns are numbered from left to right. Can you name the column where the lead story begins? Is there a story that starts in column 4? What is the headline?

FOLLOW THE LEAD: Comprehension; study skills; critical thinking; writing

(Students will need a current or day-old newspaper every day for this week-long activity.)

1. Find the lead story or another story of interest in your newspaper. Clip it out and save it in a folder.

2. Look through the newspaper and see if you can find other articles or editorials related to the news item you have selected. Cut them out and save them also.

3. Throughout the week, follow the story you have selected. Cut out and save any related articles. Can you find any editorials, letters to the editor, or political cartoons related to the story?

4. At the end of the week, put together a scrapbook of related articles. Write a short summary of the news item. Tell about any controversy over the issue. Discuss your opinions about the issue.

ABBREVIATED AD ART: Vocabulary; study skills

(Students make posters showing common abbreviations used in various types of classified ads. See Activity 1-5, page 19.)

THIS MOVE IS CLASSIFIED: Study skills

(Students use the classified ads to locate items needed after moving to a new house. See Activity 1-7, page 22.)

SPORTS PAGE SYNONYMS: Vocabulary; grammar and usage

(Students make a chart of synonyms used by sportswriters in place of common verbs. See Activity 6-2, page 163.)

MEET THE PRESS: GETTING TO KNOW THE NEWSPAPER: Comprehension; study skills

1. (Pass out a newspaper to each student. It is not necessary that they each have the same newspaper.)

2. (Have students complete Activity Sheet 8-3, page 221.)

Meet the Press: Getting to Know the Newspaper

Use a newspaper to find the following information. You will have 20 minutes to locate as many answers as you can. Be sure to use the index to help you locate information quickly.

1. Write the name and date of the newspaper. _____

   _____

2. Find the lead story. Write the headline. _____

   _____

3. Write the name of a comic strip. _____

   _____

4. Write the name of a movie being advertised in the newspaper.

   _____

5. Write the headline from a sports story. _____

   _____

6. Write the topic of a letter to the editor and the name of the

   person who wrote the letter. _____

   _____

7. Write the price, year, and make of a used car offered for sale

   in the classified ads. _____

8. Write the name of a television show that will be on at 8 p.m.

   _____

9. Write the name of a country that is written about in the

   news. _____

10. Write what tomorrow's weather will be like. _____

    _____

Let's Form a Job Club

By forming a job club or by using the ideas here, students pool their creative resources and collective talents to plan ways to earn money.

Reading/Language Arts Skills: **writing—advertisements • handwriting • spelling • creative expression • speaking—sharing experiences • drama—role playing**

Curricular Areas: **art • social studies**

Materials: **lined and unlined paper • tagboard or poster board • colored markers**

Consider doing this activity in the spring—just in time for earning summer money! And when you do it again next year, check with this year's entrepreneurs for success stories to share with the class.

PREPARATION: Announce to the class that you're willing to sponsor a job club for those who are interested in earning money from neighborhood jobs. Set a time and day for the first meeting. Since this project involves students in earning money by working outside of school, you may wish to prepare a notice for parents describing the job club and requesting permission for student participation. The notice can be distributed at the first club meeting.

DISCUSSION: How many of you sometimes earn money by working for your neighbors? What kinds of jobs do you do? How do people know you want to work and that you know how to do the job?

DIRECTIONS: (Agendas for meetings)

First Meeting:

1. (Discuss the purpose of the club. Select a name if members wish.)

2. Next, we need to decide on the best day and time for our club to meet. We'll also check the school calendar to be sure our meeting time won't conflict with other school activities.

3. Now let's brainstorm jobs you might do. I'll list them on the chalkboard.

   Some possible jobs:

   - wash windows
   - water plants or feed pets for neighbors on vacation
   - walk a dog

- baby-sit
- rent-a-party (plan games, refreshments, and prizes for a birthday party)
- do someone's shopping
- collect paper, bottles, and cans for recycling
- wash cars
- shovel snow
- mow lawns
- clean houses
- paint house numbers on front curbs
- distribute advertising fliers for a local business
- distribute campaign literature

4. Let's look at these jobs. What qualifications do you feel you would need to do the first job? (Continue discussing each job and the qualifications.)

Second Meeting:

1. (Using the list of ideas generated at the first meeting, have students choose at least one job they feel qualified for.)

2. Think about the job you would like to do. On a piece of paper, list the materials or equipment necessary to do that job. (Have some students read their lists of materials aloud.) How could we help each other get materials? (share things we have with each other; divide the list of things we need and have each person bring in one thing)

3. Now let's think of how we can advertise the services of our club members. Brainstorming is always helpful, so as you think of advertising ideas I'll list them on the chalkboard. (See Activity 5-3, "Now You're in Business," page 137, for ideas.) We also need to decide what materials are needed for our advertising and how members can help each other get them. (Continue the discussion to form a list of materials and resource possibilities. Have students plan to bring the materials to the next meeting.)

Third Meeting:

1. With the materials we have, please work on preparing your advertisements. You may work alone or with a classmate. We will work on these advertising materials today and again at our next meeting.

2. Let's think of ways to distribute our advertisements, and then decide who will be responsible for getting the advertisements out. (Be sure to obtain permission before posting the ads.)

Fourth Meeting:

1. Today we are going to complete our advertising materials.

2. (Appoint students to distribute advertising materials before the next meeting based on the last meeting's discussion.)

3. Find a friend and practice responding to people who contact you about a job.

Fifth Meeting:

1. You have been busy distributing advertising materials since our last meeting. Please share some of your experiences. What problems have you had? How did people react when you asked for permission to post announcements?

2. Have you received any requests for services? Have you finished a job? (Continue discussing responses from students on their job experiences.)

(Regular club meetings continue only as long as they serve the purpose of helping members with their jobs. Once this is accomplished, the club can be disbanded or scheduled to meet less often to share triumphs and sorrows.)

(Optional: The job club may want to sponsor a Career Day to help students become more familiar with career possibilities. See "Career Day," Project 8-5, on page 226.)

Career Day

Students use a variety of language arts skills as they plan and conduct a Career Day with guest speakers from the community.

Reading/Language Arts Skills: writing—invitations, programs, summaries, news reports • grammar and usage—sentences • mechanics of writing—capitalization and punctuation • vocabulary—content area words • spelling • listening—listening for information • speaking—making introductions, interviewing • critical thinking—expressing opinions

Curricular Areas: social studies • art

Materials: drawing paper • chart paper • pencils, markers, crayons • (optional: tape recorder and cassette • video camera and tape, VCR, television)

You'll be pleasantly surprised at how your community will rally to help. All you need to do is ask!

PREPARATION: Select a day for Career Day. Check your school calendar to be sure it won't conflict with other school activities.

DIRECTIONS: PLANNING A CAREER DAY:

1. What are some of the careers you think you might choose as adults? (List the careers on a chart.) What are some advantages as well as disadvantages of each of these careers?

2. We could invite some people in these careers to visit our class and tell us about what they do. Are there people in our community who have these careers? (Students can decide which career people they would like to invite.)

3. How could we arrange to have some of these people visit our class? (Assign each proposed guest speaker to a pair or small group of students.) Please decide how you want to contact your career person. If you plan to telephone the person or contact him or her in person, act this out in your small group. Try different ways of explaining the reason for your call or visit; then decide which approach seems most effective.

   Some of the guest speakers should be contacted in writing. Work together to draft a letter of invitation. (Invitations should be extended two to three weeks before the scheduled Career Day.)

4. (If you plan to tape the interviews on Career Day, tell students to ask the speakers for permission.)

PREPARING FOR THE SPEAKERS:

1. (Once you have determined which community members will be participating in Career Day, make a list of their names and occupations on the chalkboard.)

2. These are the speakers who will be participating in our Career Day. (Assign one or two students to interview each speaker on the list. Students may be assigned to more than one speaker.)

3. Prepare questions to ask the people you have been assigned to interview. (See Activity 5-4, "Career Connection—The Interview," page 139.)

4. (Assign one student to introduce each speaker to the class on Career Day. These students may wish to contact the speaker they will be introducing ahead of time in order to get some background information to use in the introduction.)

5. (Select a committee of students to design a printed program for Career Day. It should include the schedule for the speakers.)

ARRANGING THE ROOM:

1. (Make sure there are enough seats in the front of the room for the speakers, the students who will introduce them, and the students assigned to interview them. You may wish to have a table or podium for the speakers.)

2. (Select a few students to make name tags or cards for each speaker. These can be worn by the speakers or set on the table in front of them.)

INTRODUCING AND INTERVIEWING THE SPEAKERS:

1. (After welcoming the speakers to your class, have a student introduce the first speaker on the program. Give the speaker several minutes to talk about his or her job, then allow time for the student interviewers to ask the questions they have prepared.)

2. (Continue until each speaker has been interviewed.)

TAPING THE INTERVIEW (Optional):

(Be sure you have asked for permission in advance. Students can set up and check out the equipment ahead of time by trying it out on fellow classmates.)

REPORTING THE INTERVIEWS:

1. (Have students make a list of words relating to each career. Tell them to look up any words they're not sure of in a dictionary.)

2. (Have students write a summary of the information they learned from each speaker who spoke on Career Day. If the interviews were taped, students can use the tapes to help them.)

3. (Students can produce a Career Day News Report for the class or school. Have them include at least one item about each career. Encourage students to contribute news articles, pictures, and opinions about individual careers or about Career Day itself. Remind students to write in complete sentences and to use correct capitalization and punctuation. Students could use a computer newspaper program if one is available.)

4. (Optional) Let's critique one of the interviews. How clearly did both the speaker and the interviewer talk? Did they have voice and body mannerisms that added to or detracted from what they were saying? In what ways did they show courtesy and mutual respect?

5. (Optional: Tape one of the morning television interview shows and have the students critique it.)

THANKING THE SPEAKERS:

Don't forget to send thank-you notes to your guest speakers! (For ideas, see Activity 7-1, "Greeting Cards—Say It with Style," page 181.)

Progress Report: A Straight-*A* School

Students investigate school events and/or the use of space at school. They identify areas of strength and weakness and follow a series of problem-solving tasks to bring about improvement.

Reading/Language Arts Skills: **study skills—surveys, bar graphs, line graphs, maps • speaking— interviewing, giving a report • writing—reports • handwriting • spelling**

Curricular Areas: **social studies • mathematics • art**

Materials: **Task Cards 1-5 (pages 231-233) • chart or graph paper • markers • (optional: tape recorder and blank cassette • VCR, video camera and tape, television)**

Your students will earn high marks for improvement as they work together to build on strengths and promote a straight-A school!

PREPARATION: Meet with the school principal and discuss the project in advance. Emphasize that the focus will be on solving problems and that he or she will be kept informed at every stage of the project. Find out whether there are any problems that students could help solve.

DISCUSSION: If you were going to make out a report card for our school, which areas would get *A*'s? (playground facilities, cafeteria, music program, parent group, and so on) Why? Which areas would get lower grades? In this project, we will work on improving these areas.

When there is a problem in our city or state, how do people go about making changes? (writing to legislators, forming committees, volunteering help, voting in new laws, and so on) During your years in school, what changes or improvements have you noticed?

DIRECTIONS: Introducing the Project:

1. Let's make a list of different areas around school and events that happen (or that you'd like to see happen) at school. I'll list them on the board as you name them. (areas: office, hallways, restrooms, cafeteria, classrooms, playground, bus stop; events: Open House, assemblies, parent conferences, class parties, Grandparents' Day, talent show, and so on)

2. (Divide students into small groups.) Within your group, select an area or event from the list on the board that you would like to focus on. Each group should choose a different area or event. (You might want to distribute Task Card 1 to help students better understand what will be involved.)

3. (Assign groups to areas or events based on their preferences.) Each group is responsible for developing an improvement plan. You'll use a set of task cards to (1) Identify a Problem, (2) List Possible Solutions, (3) Select the Best Solution, (4) Test Your Solution, and (5) Make a Progress Report. Please record your findings carefully. (For activities giving practice in collecting data and graphing it, see Chapter 1, "Charts and Graphs," in *Kids Are Consumers, Too! Real-World Mathematics for Today's Classroom.*)

4. (Optional: Students may enjoy videotaping their progress reports. For tips on taped interviews, please see Activity 5-4, "Career Connection—The Interview," on page 139 and Project 8-5, "Career Day," on page 226.)

Identify a Problem

(Use with Project 8-6.)

1. Find out what problems exist in the area your group is investigating (waste, noise, litter, discipline, attendance, traffic, and so on). In order to determine what the problems are, do some or all of the following:

   - Survey students, parents, teachers, and other staff members. For example: take a poll to find out people's favorite and least favorite cafeteria foods; poll their opinions on year-round school; survey students to find out how much homework they do; and so on.
   - Make observations in the area. For example: Is it clean? Is it noisy? Is it orderly? Do people leave an assembly smiling? Which food on the tray isn't eaten?
   - Interview students, parents, teachers, and staff members. For example: ask the custodian how long it takes to scrape gum off the bottom of desks; ask teachers how school clothes worn today differ from the clothes they wore to school. (If you plan to tape the interviews, be sure to get permission beforehand.)
   - Collect data. For example: measure the amount of water lost, per minute, at a leaky water fountain; count the number of pieces of trash in an area on the playground; find out the number of parents who attended Open House in each grade level.

2. Record the information you have gathered on a chart or graph. For example: make bar graphs of everyone's favorite and least favorite cafeteria foods; draw a line graph to show the traffic in the halls at different times of the day; chart the average daily attendance of each grade in school; make a map of the schoolyard, section it off, and note pieces of trash in each portion.

List Possible Solutions

(Use with Project 8-6.)

1. Compile a list of possible solutions to the problem you have identified. Use some or all of these strategies for developing solutions:

   - Brainstorm within your group.
   - Find procedures that successfully solve similar problems in other areas of school.
   - Ask other students for possible solutions.
   - Ask parents, teachers, and other staff members for ideas.
   - Talk to people from other schools.
   - Use the library as a resource for magazine and newspaper articles that deal with the subject.

2. Within your group, narrow the list of solutions down to those ideas that seem most practical.

Select the Best Solution

(Use with Project 8-6.)

1. Make an appointment to discuss the problem and its possible solutions with your teacher or school principal. Find out if any of the solutions on your list conflict with school rules or policies. (If you plan to tape the meeting, get permission from your teacher or principal beforehand.)

2. Determine which solution students think is best. Use one of the following methods:

   - Make a ballot describing each possible solution and have all students vote.
   - Design a questionnaire for students. Find out why they prefer one solution over another.
   - Conduct a poll. Select students and faculty at random and find out which solution they prefer.

Test Your Solution

(Use with Project 8-6.)

1. Before testing your solution, get permission from your teacher or the school principal.

2. Present your solution to students and school staff members. You may want to design fliers, posters, or rule sheets describing your solution.

3. While testing your solution, keep track of problems that arise. Can the problems be taken care of, or does your solution need to be changed? Might one of your other solutions work better? Is it possible to solve the problem at this time?

4. Monitor your plan carefully. Be sure to inform appropriate staff members and students of changes that have been made in the plan. Is it efficient? Are people happy with it? Are further changes needed?

Make a Progress Report

(Use with Project 8-6.)

Prepare a group oral report on your investigation for the class and a written report for your teacher. In your progress reports you will want to:

1. Describe each step you took during your school improvement project. If you were unable to try out a solution to the problem, describe the reasons.

2. Include the positive things you noticed in the area you are reporting on.

3. Include any charts or graphs you prepared.

4. Evaluate your group's progress. Has the area been improved? Does it deserve an *A*? Why or why not?

5. If interviews were recorded, use the tapes as part of your oral report.

Part 4.
Suggestions for
Using This Book

Tips for Teachers

Using Real-World Materials

Using the Activities
    Choosing an Activity
    Planning the Activity
    Adapting Activities
    Using Activities in Related Curricular Areas
Special Features
    Quick and Easy Activities
    Real-World Reading and Language Arts
        Games

Real-World Materials
Problem-Solving Approach
Use of Computers
Activities to Do at Home
Special Uses
    Staff Development
    Substitute Teachers

Welcome to Chapter 9. (Actually, this was originally Chapter 1, but we thought you'd rather jump right into the activities—and not be bogged down with our ideas about choosing and using them.) Now that you've browsed around for a while, the ideas in this chapter may be just what you need to put this book to work.

This book is designed to be used primarily as a supplement to your reading and language arts textbooks. In addition, because of its focus on a broad range of real-world topics, this book will be useful as a supplementary resource in other areas of the curriculum, especially social studies, math, science, and even physical education. It can also be a valuable source of ideas for integrated units of study such as conservation, consumer education, and career awareness.

The content and scope of this book make it adaptable to many uses. The following section outlines some of those uses, offers ideas on how to get started, and gets specific about choosing (and changing) an activity to suit your own classroom needs. We hope you'll glance at this chapter (stopping occasionally to look back through the book for activities of particular interest to you), and then plunge ahead with real-world learning for your students.

Using the Activities

One of the most important goals we had when writing this book was to make it easy to use. The Table of Contents, the quick-reference tables following it, the charts on the inside front and back covers, and the Skills Index at the back of the book are worth getting to know—they will be your best sources of ideas to guide you to appropriate activities.

When it comes to ease of use, we think one of the best features of the book is the concise format we've used for all activities. Once you get acquainted with this format, you'll be able to glance at any activity and find just the information you want.

Although each activity is self-explanatory, we do have some general ideas about using the activities that we'd like to share with you.

Choosing an Activity. We've grouped the activities in chapters by skill areas and real-world topics. Thus, they are not arranged in a sequential order. We encourage you to select them at random, jumping around the book to find activities that suit your needs.

One good way to choose an activity is to start by finding a topic that relates to other class activities—or one that simply appeals to you. Let's assume that your fifth-grade class has been learning about different ways that people earn money and that you're emphasizing following directions. A quick glance at the Table of Contents suggests that a good topic would be Careers, Jobs, and Chores (Chapter 5). As you turn to this chapter, you look for activities that include following directions at the fifth-grade level (shown in the grade level indicator at the top of the page). When you thumb through the chapter, you'll see that Activities 5, 6, and 8 all include following directions at the fifth grade level. By reading the brief descriptions of these activities, you can select one (or more) that suits your needs.

Another quick way to locate activities that provide practice in specific skills is to look in the Skills Index at the back of the book. For example, if you have been teaching about compound words, you'll find several activities on compound words in the Skills Index under Vocabulary.

Many activities can be adapted to cover a wide span of achievement, and thus are indicated for many grade levels. For instance, Activity 5-3, "Now You're in Business," is recommended for grades 3 through 8. If this is the activity you choose, you can select one or several of the activities under DIRECTIONS that involve reading and language arts skills at the level your students can handle.

Once you find an activity that fits the topic and skills you need, you can adjust the level of difficulty to make it just right for your students: change the vocabulary, vary the difficulty of discussion questions, omit some of the steps, or include one of the variations.

Planning the Activity. Once you've chosen an activity, the next step is to see what's suggested for MATERIALS and PREPARATION. Most of the printed materials that you'll need are included right with the activity. Page numbers are always indicated so that materials located elsewhere in the book are also easy to find.

Some of the real-world materials included in the book require prices on them. On most of these, we've left blank spaces for you to fill in with appropriate prices. By filling in your own prices, you can always have current, realistic lessons. Regardless of what happens to the price of cars, tennis balls, or even pancakes, your real-world materials will be up to date!

The MATERIALS section lists other supplies in addition to the printed items needed for the activity. You'll be able to find most of these items in your classroom supply closet. Sometimes we've suggested additional materials such as newspapers, empty supermarket containers, and travel brochures that are easy to obtain from local sources. Chapter 10 includes suggestions for obtaining such materials.

Another step in planning an activity is deciding how to group your students. Most of the activities are designed to be used with the whole class, but they're equally useful for smaller groups. Other activities, such as games, are designed for small groups. In most of these cases, it's a simple matter to divide the whole class into small groups and let them all play the game at the same time.

A few activities consist of Task Cards to be used in learning stations. There are also some activities that work best for independent study. These can be made available at an interest table or as part of a learning station.

As you can see, there's a lot of flexibility in the ways you can use these activities. We encourage you to let your plans reflect your own style so that you'll enjoy these real-world activities as much as your students do.

Adapting Activities. If your class is typical, your students will have a wide range of abilities. One of the strengths of the activities in this book is that they can easily be adapted to different levels of difficulty. There are several ways to do this:

- Choose only part of an activity
- Vary the difficulty of the vocabulary
- Vary the writing tools used (pencil and paper, typewriter, word processor)
- Emphasize different skills
- Vary the level of questions

Another feature of these activities is that many of them can be used more than once. There are several good reasons for doing this:

- For repeated practice in the same skill
- For increasingly difficult practice in a skill
- For application of a skill in a different context

When you repeat an activity, it doesn't have to be exactly the same each time. You can give it a new twist by:

- Including one of the VARIATIONS
- Changing the topic or context
- Using a different set of real-world materials (such as catalogs from a different store or menus from a different restaurant)

Once you find activities that are particularly appealing to your students, you may discover that they become a familiar part of your daily program. And we all know how much children enjoy repeating their favorite games and activities over . . . and over . . . and over!

Using Activities in Related Curricular Areas. Although the main focus of this book is reading and language arts, most of the activities can be used in other curricular areas. For instance, as a social studies lesson you might want to use "Patent Pending" (Chapter 5); a good math activity would be "It Pays to Advertise" (Chapter 2); "Greeting Cards—Say It with Style" (Chapter 7) could be used for an art lesson.

Because your school schedule is so crowded, you may be searching for ways to use time more effectively. One easy way to cover more bases during your busy day is to combine the time allotted for two different curricular areas, such as language arts and social studies. Then you can choose a real-world activity that fits both these areas, such as "Way to Go!" (Chapter 6). Students will then experience how skills needed in the real world require different kinds of learning.

To make it easier for you to find appropriate activities, we've included a matrix on page xi that shows curricular areas related to each activity.

Special Features

We've included a number of special features to make this book as flexible and useful as possible.

Quick and Easy Activities. Do you sometimes need an appealing, quick and easy activity to fill the last few minutes before lunch? Do you ever have some restless moments before the last bus arrives? Every activity chapter has Quick and Easy activities that are designed just for those times. We suggest you look them over and mark several that are especially appealing to you. Then, when those free minutes occur, you'll be ready with a catchy activity that's just right for your class.

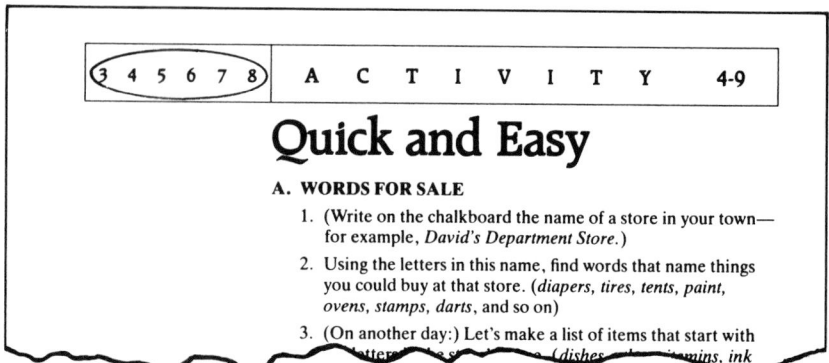

Most of the Quick and Easy activities can be used over and over.
For some of them, you can change the questions slightly by asking
for a different type of word or a different sentence structure. For
example, use adjectives instead of verbs, two-syllable words instead
of one, and so on. For other activities, you can repeat the same
question but use a different content or theme. For example, if
students alphabetize types of seeds on one day, another day they
can alphabetize spices, canned soups, or sports equipment.

Real-World Reading and Language Arts Games. Games can be a
very effective way to practice reading and language arts skills. For
that reason, we've included at least one game in each chapter. The
list on the inside back cover is a handy reference for finding them.

Real-World Materials. Using real-world materials is an important and exciting part of real-world reading and language arts. You may want to plan activities around certain real-world materials. You can scan the Real-World Materials Chart on the inside front cover (repeated on page 255) to get a general idea of inexpensive and easy-to-obtain materials you can use. Then look in Chapter 10, starting on page 256, for some specific suggestions for using these materials.

Problem-Solving Approach. We've made a special effort to apply reading and language arts skills to realistic situations as diverse as writing letters to the editor, critiquing television shows, and reading warranties. When your students do these critical thinking activities, they have to consider the following:

- What am I trying to find out?
- What information do I have?
- Do I have enough information?
- How can I get additional information?
- How do I use this information to solve the problem?
- What is my opinion on the subject?
- Is my presentation clear and reasonable?

Use of Computers. The use of computers in the classroom continues to undergo rapid change. Because of this we have included computers as useful, but not essential, tools of language arts instruction. We have included suggestions related to word processing, data-base management, and computer literacy.

Word processing is sometimes suggested as a way to vary an activity. It is particularly useful when students are going through several stages of writing and rewriting and when the same or similar text, such as a form letter, needs to be generated.

Activities to Do at Home. One of the underlying themes of this book is to promote good relations between home and school. We encourage you to take advantage of opportunities to convey positive messages while you're teaching real-world reading and language arts skills.

For some activities, students collect data at home—such as the family's preferences for television programs or breakfast cereals. For other activities, students may be asked to bring materials or supplies to class, such as catalogs, magazines, or empty cereal boxes.

Such interactions will help parents and other adults understand that homework can be much more than just spelling practice. They'll also get a better idea of what's going on at school—and they'll be delighted to see that their children are learning the real-world skills that will help them become wise consumers.

Special Uses

In the previous pages, we have shared ideas for teachers who are using this book in their regular classrooms. In this section, we'll highlight some other uses.

Staff Development. We think the book can be especially useful to curriculum specialists, resource teachers, principals, and others who have responsibility for continuing professional development in their schools. In a workshop setting, real-world reading and language arts activities can be used very effectively to achieve several important goals:

- To provide teachers with examples of effective activities
- To give teachers a chance to experience activities before introducing them in their classes
- To provide the kind of information and support teachers need in their ongoing efforts to improve instructional programs and procedures

Substitute Teachers. We hope that substitute teachers will find this book especially useful. More and more, substitutes are carrying their own bags of plans with them—to avoid the situations that can occur when regular lesson plans aren't available or don't work. Real-world reading and language arts activities can be particularly effective for the following reasons:

- They are highly motivating to students.
- They can be adapted to different levels of difficulty.
- They provide opportunities to practice as well as to apply reading and language arts skills.

You can provide yourself with a set of flexible lesson plans by putting together the following materials:

- Thirty copies of cereal boxes (Activities 1-1, 1-2, 4-5)
- Thirty copies of ad pages and invoices (Activity 6-4)
- A set of 30 phone book yellow pages and 30 message forms (Activities 3-1, 4-4)
- A collection of newspapers (for activities, see page 266)
- Two sets of game boards (page 277)—one set blank, one set filled in (for games, see the chart on the inside back cover)

With these few basic materials and some well-thought-out lesson plans, you'll be all set for that 6:00 a.m. phone call!

We've put our best efforts together to write a book that combines exciting real-world activities, an easy-to-use format, and an awareness of the uniqueness of every individual. We hope that you will find this book to be an ideal resource for helping your students learn about the real world of reading and language arts.

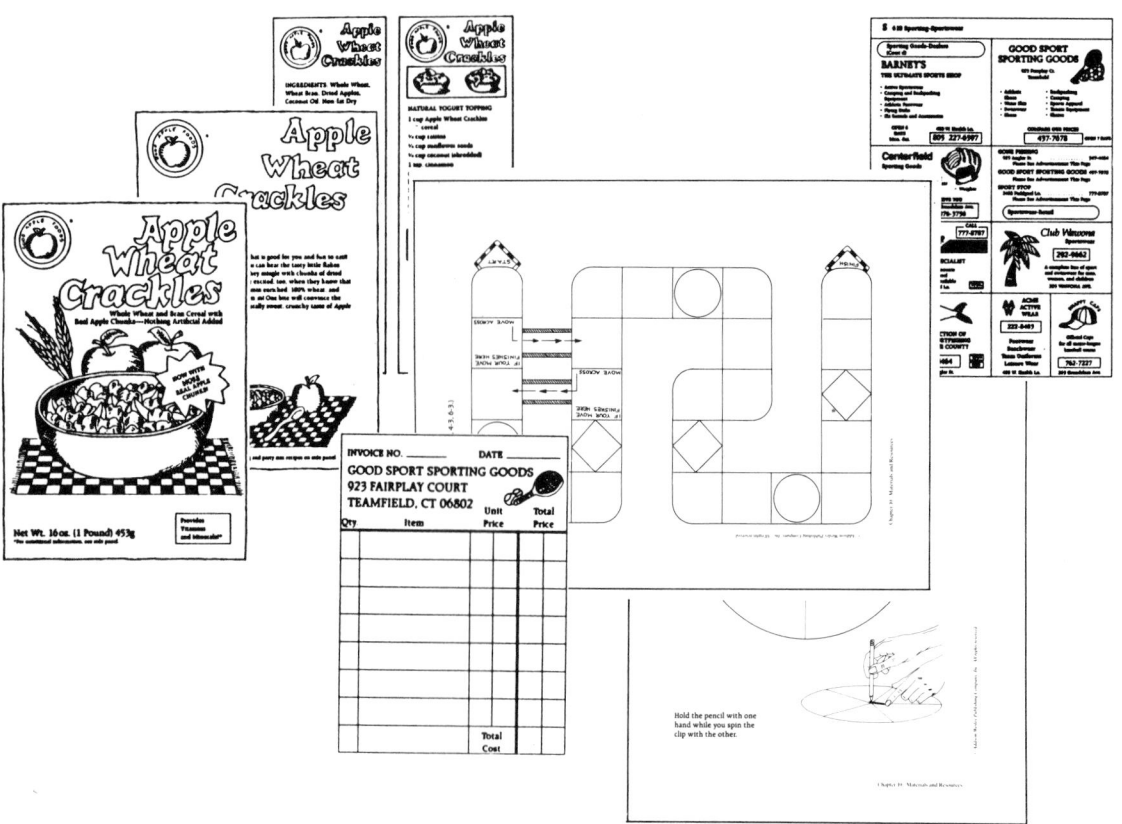

Part 5.
Materials and
Resources

Materials and Resources

Making Real-World Games

General Suggestions for Materials and Resources

  Ways to Get Materials
  Ways to Use Materials
  Guest Speakers
  Field Trips
  An Alternative to Guest Speakers and Field Trips

Real-World Materials Chart

Specific Suggestions for Materials and Resources

Real-World Games Chart

Teaching Aids

Award Certificates

Song

Letters, lists, ads, and applications—we deal with a wide variety of real-world materials every day. And because real-world reading and language arts is what this book is all about, it, too, deals with a variety of materials.

To save you time, we've included many authentic-looking items throughout the book. (See the chart on the inside front cover.) You can find a menu, a yellow page from the telephone book, package labels, and catalog order forms. But you can add even more realism by using items from places right in your own community, such as menus from local restaurants, pages from your local telephone book, and package labels from products students bring from home.

Included in this chapter are some hints about ways to get materials from local sources, ways to use materials (your materials as well as ours), guest speakers, and field trips. We've even thrown in a suggestion for using telephone technology as an inexpensive alternative to a guest speaker or a field trip!

At the end of the chapter, you'll find award certificates, which can be duplicated and given to individual students during the year and also used for an end-of-year ceremony.

We hope these materials are just the magic ingredient you need to help your students enjoy reading and language arts while they experience and solve realistic real-world problems.

General Suggestions for Materials and Resources

There are a variety of ways for you to obtain and use materials and resources to bring real-world reading and language arts to your classroom. This section contains a few general suggestions just to get you started.

Ways to Get Materials. The following are tried and true ways to obtain materials with a minimum of trouble and expense.

- Ask students' families to help by saving and donating materials. The sample letter on page 251 may be helpful. Or, if students write the letter, it might turn out even better— resulting in more materials *and* more writing experience. If you have a computer, save the letters—yours and the students'—on the word processor to revise as needed.

- Request items in writing from local businesses. And don't forget to use school stationery. It works every time! In fact, your school secretary may be willing to type your letters for you. The sample letter on page 252 may help you. Follow-up phone calls made by students may help, too.
- Many times the easiest way is to collect materials here and there a little at a time. When you have enough of a certain item, which may be next month or next year (!), you'll be ready to do the activity.
- If you can get only one copy of a particular item, duplicate it to make a copy for each student.
- A very important thought: *Sharing materials with your fellow teachers saves time!* If you collect menus . . . and another teacher gets some maps . . . and then you share . . . you've each cut your time in half. Of course, if you get a third teacher to pick up some job applications. . . .

SAMPLE LETTER TO FAMILY

Dear Family:

Our class will soon be studying ———————————.
In order to do some real-world activities about this topic, we will be using some extra materials.

We would really appreciate your help. Would you please save your ————————————————————
and send them to school with your child? We need them by
————————————————.

Thanks for your help.

Sincerely,

————————————————

SAMPLE LETTER TO BUSINESSES

(Use school stationery if possible.)

Dear _____ :

Our class will soon be studying _____ .
In order to do some real-world activities about this topic, we
need some extra materials.

Please help us. Would you donate _____ ?
We would be glad to pick them up at your convenience. We
need them by _____ .

I will be calling you on _____ to answer any
questions you may have. If you would like to talk to me before
that, please call me at _____ .

Thank you for your help.

Sincerely,

_____

Ways to Use Materials. See the Real-World Materials Chart on
page 255 and the inside front cover. This chart lists materials that
are in this book and the pages where they're found, as well as
materials that are easy to obtain locally. You can often substitute
items from local firms for the materials we've given you in the book.

If you laminate or cover your materials with clear contact paper,
they'll last much longer. Generally speaking, this is a good in-
vestment of your time and energy; however, in some cases, this
covering may take away from the authentic look of the materials.

Many materials can be made into transparencies and used with an
overhead projector. Having ads, maps, menus, newspapers, and

other such materials available for the overhead makes it possible to get the whole class involved in discussions related to these real-world topics.

Guest Speakers. Having guest speakers come to the classroom to share information, experiences, and dreams can spark days of anticipation and excitement in your class. Here are some thoughts we hope will be of help to you:

- Parents and grandparents are excellent resources as guest speakers.
- Alumni of the school are also good resources.
- Many companies have public relations personnel who would be delighted to come to your school. It's good public relations for the business—and a great experience for your class.
- Check with your local chamber of commerce. They often keep a file of business people who are willing to speak to school groups.
- When you and your class have chosen a guest speaker, have your students decide what questions they want to ask. Have them write the questions down. Then, when you call to make arrangements with the speaker, you can share this list of questions.
- A detailed plan for preparing your class for a visit from a guest speaker is described in Activity 5-4, "Career Connection—The Interview," page 139. Also, Project 8-5, "Career Day," page 226, focuses on guest speakers from local businesses.

Field Trips. Do you remember going on field trips when you were young? We do. And they stand out as important events in our school experiences. Even though it may only have been a class walk to the corner store, a restaurant, or a bank, the lasting impression made by that learning experience is seldom duplicated by any other school experience. Here are some ideas to keep in mind as you plan a field trip:

- Involve your students in choosing a place to go and planning the trip.
- Local businesses and industries are excellent places to visit. Sometimes they are as close as a phone call and a leisurely walk! If you telephone a local fast-food restaurant, a super-market, or even a newspaper office, and ask them to help you help youngsters . . . they're sure to cooperate.

- When you call to make arrangements, be prepared to explain the purpose of the trip and the kinds of things the students will be looking for. Ask the manager to greet the students and give a short talk (three to five minutes) to acquaint them with the store, restaurant, or business.
- After the field trip, use some class time to share ideas about what was seen and learned. Students can write thank-you notes to the person who arranged the visit as well as to other people who were especially helpful. Encourage students to describe one special thing they learned or enjoyed on the trip. For thank-you note ideas, see Activity 7-1, "Greeting Cards—Say It with Style," page 181.

An Alternative to Guest Speakers and Field Trips. With the help of a speaker phone hooked into a room large enough to hold your class—or with help from your local telephone company, who will hook up a phone in your classroom—your entire class can talk to a busy newspaper reporter, a far-off senator, even a famous celebrity, or someone else who would otherwise not have the time to come to your class.

The telephone company has equipment that will amplify the sound of the person's voice so that the whole class can hear it. They can also provide equipment that allows the students to talk to the speaker from anywhere in the room. The bad news is that you'll have to schedule this far in advance. The good news is that the service is usually free! (See Guest Speakers and Field Trips above for additional suggestions.)

Real-World Materials Chart. The following chart lists—in alphabetical order—the real-world materials needed for the activities in this book. The chart tells you which activities use each of the materials and gives page numbers of blackline masters for materials provided in the text. It also gives page numbers of specific suggestions regarding each of the materials. These page numbers refer to the following section, Specific Suggestions for Materials and Resources, which lists the materials in the same order as the chart and suggests ways of obtaining and using each material along with suggestions for related guest speakers and field trips. For easy reference, the chart is repeated on the inside front cover.

Real-World Materials Chart

Materials	Blackline Master (page)	Activity or Project Number	Specific Suggestions (page)
1. Advertisements (classified ads, forms, sporting goods ads, food ads)	47 and 169	1-5, 1-7, 2-2, 4-7, 6-4, 7-6, 8-3	256
2. Audio-Visual Materials (videotape, radio, records, song lyrics, cassettes)	280	3-5, 3-6, 5-3, 8-2, 8-5, 8-6	257
3. Catalogs (page and order form)	105 and 106	1-3, 2-3, 4-2, 6-6	258
4. Cereal Boxes	9, 10, and 11	1-1, 1-2, 4-5	259
5. Certificates (gift certificate, patent/inventor forms; see also Warranties)	107 and 135	4-2, 5-2, 7-5	260
6. Greeting Cards and Decorations (see also telegrams)	183, 184, 185, 186, 191, and 192	7-1, 7-3	261
7. Invoices	170	6-4	262
8. Job-hunting Items (applications, résumés, business cards)	143 and 147	5-3, 5-5, 5-6	263
9. Labels and Packaging (cereal boxes and other containers and labels)	9, 10, and 11	1-1, 1-2, 1-4*, 2-4, 2-5*, 4-5	264
10. Magazines	#	1-6, 3-2, 4-7, 6-6, 7-4, 7-6, 8-2	265
11. Maps	175	6-7	266
12. Newspapers (see also Advertisements)	#	1-5, 1-7, 3-2, 6-1, 6-2, 7-6, 8-3	266
13. Recipes	27	1-8, 7-5*	267
14. Restaurant Items (menus and order forms)	101 and 102	4-1	268
15. Supermarket Items (see also Labels and Packaging)	9, 10, and 11	1-1, 1-2, 1-4*, 2-4, 2-5*, 4-5	269
16. Telegrams	211 and 212	8-1	270
17. Telephone Items (white and yellow phone book pages, message forms)	77 and 113	2-7, 3-1, 4-4	270
18. Television Schedules	#	6-3	271
19. Travel Brochures	35 and 36	1-10*	272
20. Warranties (See also Certificates)	31	1-9*	273

\# Easy to obtain locally

* This activity does not require the use of the listed material, but using it might enhance the real-world nature of the activity.

Specific Suggestions for Materials and Resources

This section is a treasure-trove of ideas for enriching your reading and language arts classes with the items and resources in the materials chart. We invite you to use these inexpensive, easy-to-obtain, and very interesting materials and resources in the activities and projects we've outlined in Chapters 1 through 8—but don't stop there! Use your imagination and invent your own real-world activities.

1. ADVERTISEMENTS

    A. Ways to Get Materials:

        1. Use the ads on page 169 and the classified ad form on page 47.

        2. Magazines, newspapers, or weekly shopping ads are a great source of advertisements printed in a style that can be easily duplicated. For ways to get a classroom set of newspapers so that everyone in class can have the same set of advertisements, see NEWSPAPERS (12) below.

        3. If you're a camera buff, take some pictures (slides) of various advertisements, billboards, and store windows around town. You'll definitely have the attention of your class when you use them to start a language arts or reading lesson. Ask questions about the way words are used, the adjectives that are chosen, and how facts and opinions are expressed.

    B. Ways to Use Materials:

        1. Please see

Activity 1-5	Abbreviated Ad Art	page 19
Activity 1-7	This Move Is Classified	page 22
Activity 2-2	It Pays to Advertise	page 45
Activity 4-7	Old and Neglected Ads	page 122
Activity 6-4	Good Sport Sporting Goods	page 167
Activity 7-6	A Holiday Feast	page 199
Activity 8-3	Meet the Press: Getting to Know the Newspaper	page 219

        2. If you are going to duplicate more than one page of ads, run them off on different colors of paper to help keep them separate.

C. *Guest Speakers:* Advertising executive; commercial artist; local newspaper's advertising staff; salesperson.

D. *Field Trips:* Local newspaper; neighborhood walk to look at billboards and other forms of advertising.

2. AUDIO-VISUAL MATERIALS

A. *Ways to Get Materials:*

1. Borrow a tape recorder or, if possible, a video camera and VCR; then tape radio and television commercials at home.

2. Students or their parents are often eager and willing to tape commercials using their home equipment.

3. Ask students to bring records or tapes of their favorite music to school. You may want to use the sample letter to families on page 251 for this.

B. *Ways to Use Materials:*

1. Please see

Activity 3-5	Tune In to Feelings	page 84
Activity 3-6	Meaningful Music	page 85
Activity 5-3	Now You're in Business!	page 137
Project 8-2	Let's Advertise Nationwide	page 213
Project 8-5	Career Day	page 226
Project 8-6	Progress Report: A Straight-*A* School	page 229

2. Use a video camera to tape oral presentations by students. Compare student presentations with presentations recorded from television. In what ways are the presentations alike? Different? In what respects should they be similar? Different?

3. Tape commercials from the radio or television. Discuss the use of action verbs, adjectives, rhyming words, and so on. What makes one commercial or jingle more appealing than another?

4. After listening to a recording of a popular song, have students design an album cover that conveys that song's message.

C. *Guest Speakers:* Advertising executive; professional lecturer; songwriter; disc jockey; record salesperson.

D. *Field Trips:* Local radio or televison station; record store.

3. CATALOGS

A. *Ways to Get Materials:*

1. Use the catalog page and order form on pages 105 and 106.

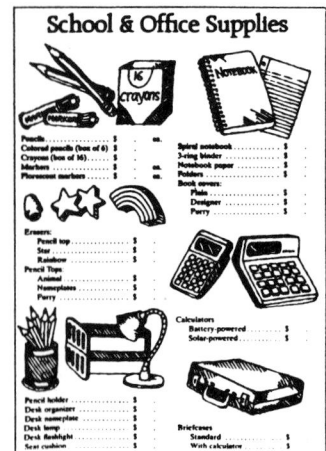
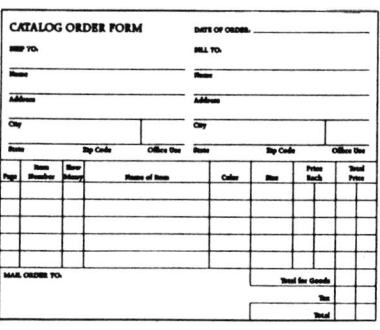

2. If you want a set of catalogs from a mail order company, find out when their current one is going to expire. Then ask the catalog store if they will save the old ones for you when the new issue comes out. If you tell them they'll be used to teach kids reading and language arts skills . . . they won't be able to resist.

3. Ask parents to save their catalogs for you. Use the sample letter on page 251.

4. Duplicate one or more catalog pages for every student.

B. *Ways to Use Materials:*

1. Please see

Activity 1-3	Index Treasure Hunt	page 15
Activity 2-3	Create-a-Catalog	page 49
Activity 4-2	Pick a Present for a Pal	page 103
Activity 6-6	Let It Snow!	page 172

C. *Guest Speakers:* Catalog store manager; order clerk or others who process mail orders; warehouse employee.

D. *Field Trips:* Local catalog store; mail order warehouse.

4. CEREAL BOXES

A. *Ways to Get Materials:*

1. Use the cereal box front, back, and sides on pages 9, 10 and 11.

  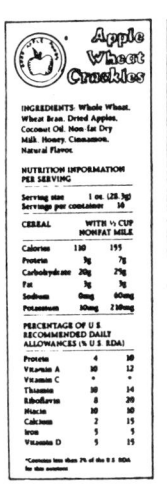 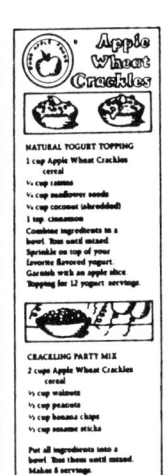

2. Ask students to save empty cereal boxes and bring them from home. Suggest that they open cereal boxes from the bottom, so that the empty container looks unopened when it sits on a desk or shelf.

3. Have students design their own cereal boxes.

B. *Ways to Use Materials:*

1. Please see

Activity 1-1	Reading Apple Wheat Crackles	page 5
Activity 1-2	An *A* to *Z* Activity	page 13
Activity 4-5	Name, Rank, and Cereal Number	page 115

2. Have students look for abbreviations, proper nouns, compound words, adjectives, and so forth on cereal boxes.

C. *Guest Speakers:* Supermarket manager; nutritionist; commercial artist.

D. *Field Trips:* Supermarket; health food store; packaging company.

5. CERTIFICATES

A. *Ways to Get Materials:*

1. Use the gift certificate on page 107 and the Inventor's Oath form and Patent Certificate on page 135.

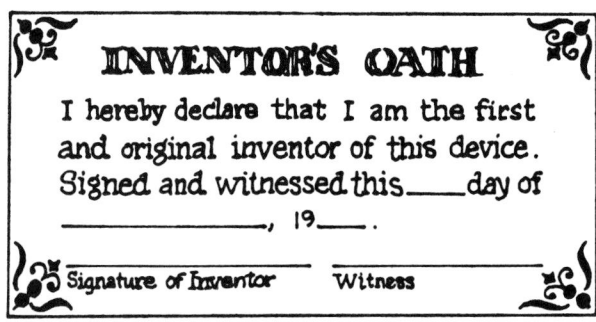

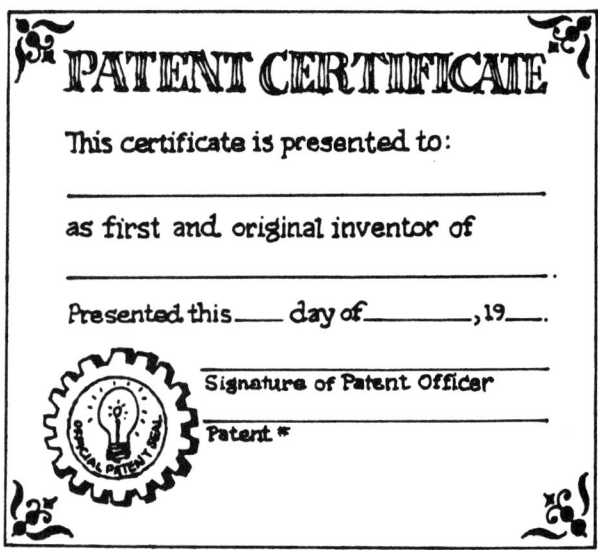

2. Make an overhead transparency or photocopies of a single gift certificate.

B. *Ways to Use Materials:*

1. Please see

Activity 4-2	Pick a Present for a Pal	page 103
Activity 5-2	Patent Pending	page 134
Activity 7-5	So It's Your Birthday	page 194

C. *Guest Speakers:* Appliance sales or repair person; inventor.

D. *Field Trips:* Appliance store; hardware store; gadget section of a department store.

6. GREETING CARDS AND DECORATIONS

A. *Ways to Get Materials:*

1. Use the directions for a pop-up card on page 183 and the greeting cards on pages 184, 185, and 186. Use the decorations on pages 191 and 192.

2. Ask parents to save old greeting cards for you. Use the sample letter on page 251. For best results, send your requests home right before holidays.

3. Ask friends, neighbors, and fellow teachers to save cards for you.

B. *Ways to Use Materials:*

1. Please see

Activity 7-1	Greeting Cards—Say It with Style	page 181
Activity 7-3	Poet-Tree and Other Decorations	page 188

2. Paper chain decorations can be used as a way of keeping track of the number of books read by class members. As students finish reading a book, have them write the book title and author and their own name on a strip of paper. The strip can be added as a link on a class chain. For a school-wide reading project, classes can combine their chains and link them around the cafeteria. As the chain grows, so will students' enthusiasm for reading.

C. *Guest Speakers:* Commercial artist; card company sales representative.

D. *Field Trips:* Local greeting card store; greeting card manufacturer.

7. INVOICES

A. *Ways to Get Materials:*

1. Use the blank invoices on page 170.

```
┌─────────────────────────────────────────┐
│ INVOICE NO. _____     DATE _____       │
│ GOOD SPORT SPORTING GOODS                │
│ 923 FAIRPLAY COURT                       │
│ TEAMFIELD, CT 06802   Unit    Total      │
│ Qty.       Item       Price   Price      │
│                                          │
│                                          │
│                                          │
│                                          │
│                                          │
│                                          │
│                                          │
│                       Total              │
│                       Cost               │
└─────────────────────────────────────────┘
```

2. You can purchase a pad of 100 blank invoices at your local variety store, discount store, or drug store. You can also get some that local stores actually use—many times with their names printed on them. Duplicate the invoices if you don't have enough to go around.

3. School invoices or purchase orders showing supplies ordered for your school or class will be especially interesting to your students.

B. *Ways to Use Materials:*

1. Please see

Activity 6-4   Good Sport Sporting Goods   page 167

2. Make copies of the invoices on page 170. Have students order items from a local sporting goods store advertisement.

C. *Guest Speakers:* Clerk from a local store; store manager.

D. *Field Trips:* Department store; specialty stores.

8. JOB-HUNTING ITEMS

A. *Ways to Get Materials:*

1. Use the job application form on page 143 and the résumé form on page 147.

Step to Success—Write a Résumé

Résumé

NAME:

ADDRESS:

TELEPHONE:

EDUCATION:
(Include the name and city of each school attended. List the school most recently attended first.)

WORK EXPERIENCE:
(List the job most recently held first. Include a brief explanation of your work responsibilities.)

VOLUNTEER EXPERIENCE:
(Include school and community involvement.)

HOBBIES AND INTERESTS:

OTHER INFORMATION:
(Include any special awards you've received.)

PITTS-BURGERS JOB APPLICATION

PLEASE PRINT — An Equal Opportunity Employer

| TODAY'S DATE | NAME (FIRST, MIDDLE, LAST) | | SOCIAL SECURITY NO. | PHONE NO. |

| ADDRESS (NUMBER, STREET, CITY, STATE, AND ZIP) | | IN EMERGENCY, NOTIFY (NAME, ADDRESS) | | PHONE NO. |

| SCHOOL ATTENDING, CITY, STATE | | GRADE | EXTRA-CURRICULAR ACTIVITIES |

WORK HISTORY Enter below your last two positions held. Start with the most recent; include any volunteer experience.

Dates From	Through	Company Name and Address	Position Held	Reason for Leaving

DETAILS OF WORK WANTED

| For what job are you applying? | Part Time ☐ | Full Time ☐ | Hours Available | SUN. | MON. | TUES. | WED. | THURS. | FRI. | SAT. |

REFERENCES: PLEASE LIST THE NAMES OF THREE PEOPLE WHO HAVE KNOWN YOU FOR AT LEAST ONE YEAR (EXCLUDING RELATIVES).

| NAME | RELATIONSHIP | PHONE NO. | COMMENTS (FOR OFFICE USE ONLY) |

Please add your signature in the space provided.

Signature _____ Date _____

THANK YOU FOR YOUR TIME AND EFFORT AND FOR YOUR INTEREST IN WORKING AT PITTS-BURGERS

2. Ask local businesses for copies of the applications they hand out to potential employees. They will usually give you all you need.

3. Blank job applications can be purchased at stationery or office supply stores.

4. Make an overhead transparency of your own résumé or that of a friend to use as a model for students.

5. Collect sample business cards from local business people or ask students to bring in a business card from a parent, relative, or friend.

B. *Ways to Use Materials:*

1. Please see

Activity 5-3	Now You're in Business!	page 137
Activity 5-5	Apply Yourself—Get a Job!	page 141
Activity 5-6	Step to Success—Write a Résumé	page 145

C. *Guest Speakers:* Manager of a local business that employs young people (fast-food restaurant, movie theater, newspaper circulation department, and so on); worker in your local employment or unemployment office; counselor from a local college job placement office.

D. *Field Trips:* Employment office; local businesses.

9. LABELS AND PACKAGING

A. *Ways to Get Materials:*

1. Use the cereal box front, back, and sides on pages 9–11.
2. Save labels from bottles, boxes, and packages. Look for clear, crisp labels that will be easy to duplicate.
3. Have students bring labels and empty packages from home. Use the sample letter on page 251. It adds fun and authenticity if boxes and cans are opened from the bottom. Then when they sit on a table or shelf the packages look unopened.

B. *Ways to Use Materials:*

1. Please see

Activity 1-1	Reading Apple Wheat Crackles	page 5
Activity 1-2	An *A* to *Z* Activity	page 13
Activity 1-4	Message on a Bottle	page 16
Activity 2-4	To Whom It May Concern	page 51
Activity 2-5	For a Code, Take Lemon Syrup	page 53
Activity 4-5	Name, Rank, and Cereal Number	page 115

2. Have students design their own labels. Then make up vocabulary or reading questions based on the labels.

C. *Guest Speakers:* Supermarket manager; pharmacist or drug store manager.

D. *Field Trips:* Variety store; drug store; health food store; supermarket.

10. MAGAZINES

A. *Ways to Get Materials:*

1. The first place to try is your own attic, basement, or storage room!

2. The second place to try is your friend's, neighbor's, or cousin Ernie's attic, basement, or storage room.

3. For a third try—ask parents. See the sample letter on page 251.

B. *Ways to Use Materials:*

1. Please see

Activity 1-6	Monitoring Your Magazine	page 20
Activity 3-2	A Picture Is Worth a Thousand Words	page 79
Activity 4-7	Old and Neglected Ads	page 122
Activity 6-6	Let It Snow!	page 172
Activity 7-4	Cut-Ups!	page 193
Activity 7-6	A Holiday Feast	page 199
Activity 8-2	Let's Advertise Nationwide	page 213

2. Always keep a stack of magazines on hand. They make great reading material—as well as a terrific source of pictures to cut out for word collages and other language arts or reading projects.

C. *Guest Speakers:* Commercial artist; local magazine staff member; magazine executive; photographer.

D. *Field Trips:* Magazine offices; printing company.

11. MAPS

A. *Ways to Get Materials:*

1. Use the city map on page 175.

2. A real estate office, the chamber of commerce, or the automobile association are all great sources for maps of your hometown. If you'd like a large wall map of your city, contact the office of city planning or the Census Bureau.

3. If you want everyone to use the same map, duplicate the portion you would like to use in class.

B. *Ways to Use Materials:*

1. Please see

   Activity 6-7   Way to Go!   page 173

2. Have students use a map to practice giving and following directions.

C. *Guest Speakers:* Automobile association personnel; a colleague or friend who's a map enthusiast.

D. *Field Trips:* Automobile association; neighborhood walk to look at the lay of the land in relationship to a map.

12. NEWSPAPERS

A. *Ways to Get Materials:*

1. Day-old newspapers are easy to get. Ask the local newspaper if they'll save yesterday's paper for you. Since a lot of activities work well when two or three students share one newspaper, you don't always need a full class set.

2. Duplicate a part of the newspaper so that everyone in the class can have a copy of the same section.

B. *Ways to Use Materials:*

1. Please see

   Activity 1-5   Abbreviated Ad Art   page 19
   Activity 1-7   This Move Is Classified   page 22

Activity 3-2   A Picture Is Worth   page 79
              a Thousand Words

Activity 6-1   Comic Strip Punctuation   page 159

Activity 6-2   Sports Page Synonyms   page 163

Activity 7-6   A Holiday Feast   page 199

Activity 8-3   Meet the Press: Getting   page 219
              to Know the Newspaper

2. Give each student a newspaper page and ask them to go on a treasure hunt for compound words, rhyming words, adjectives, proper nouns, homonyms, synonyms, and so on.

C. *Guest Speakers:* Advertising executive; cartoonist; journalist; local newspaper staff member; photographer.

D. *Field Trips:* Local newspaper; advertising agency.

13. RECIPES

A. *Ways to Get Materials:*

1. Use the recipe for soft pretzels on page 27.

2. Use any cookbook. (Students might find it interesting if you use a collection of recipes published by a local club or community service organization.)

3. Ask your students to bring their favorite recipes from home. (See the sample letter on page 251.)

B. *Ways to Use Materials:*

1. Please see

   Activity 1-8   A Twisted Memory Teaser   page 25

   Activity 7-5   So It's Your Birthday   page 194

2. Use students' favorite recipes from home to compile and publish a class cookbook.

3. Have students experiment with a format for recipes using either a database or a word processor.

4. Make a copy of a recipe on an overhead projector transparency. Ask sequencing questions. (What do you do first? What do you do after adding the eggs? What do you do before pouring the batter into the pan?)

C. *Guest Speakers:* Caterer; chef; short-order cook; school cafeteria worker; a grandparent who loves to cook(!).

D. *Field Trips:* Bakery; catering shop; restaurant; school cafeteria.

14. RESTAURANT ITEMS

A. *Ways to Get Materials:*

1. Use the menu and order forms on pages 101 and 102.

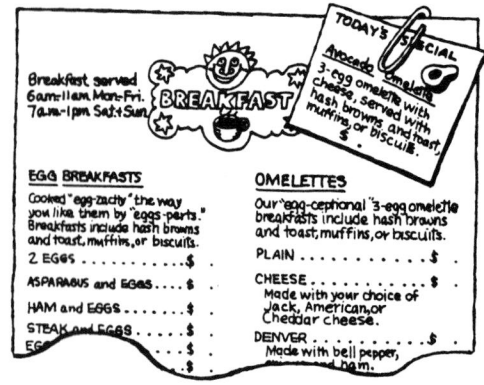 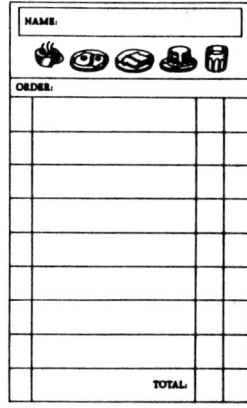

2. Take-out or travel menus from local restaurants are easy to get—especially if you say the magic words, "Help me help kids!" And don't forget to ask for a pad of the blank order forms on which the food orders are written.

3. Some restaurants have all or part of their menu printed on paper placemats. Get one for each student's desk to make a lesson especially fun.

4. If you have only one copy of the menu you want, duplicate it for the class. Colored paper makes it look more realistic. You can have students paste the menu on a piece of construction paper and then fold it over to make an attractive cover.

B. *Ways to Use Materials:*

1. Please see

   Activity 4-1   Good Eating Reading   page 99

C. *Guest Speakers:* Cook; maitre d'; restaurant owner; waiter or waitress.

D. *Field Trips:* Local restaurant; restaurant supply house.

15. SUPERMARKET ITEMS

A. *Ways to Get Materials:*

1. Use the cereal box front, back, and sides on pages 9, 10, and 11.

2. You can easily get empty bottles, boxes, and cans by putting out a call to parents. Use the sample letter on page 251. Ask them to open the bottoms of the packages when removing the contents. This way the empty container looks unopened when its sits on a shelf.

3. Newspapers are a great source of food advertisements that are printed in a style that is easy to duplicate. For ways to get a classroom set of newspapers, see NEWSPAPERS (12) above.

4. Do you have a camera? You'll really have your students' attention if you take pictures (slides) of various shelves and sections of a local supermarket. You can ask questions about the placement of items on the shelves, package design, or even the kinds of conversations that occur in the supermarket aisles!

B. *Ways to Use Materials:*

1. Please see

Activity 1-1	Reading Apple Wheat Crackles	page 5
Activity 1-2	An *A* to *Z* Activity	page 13
Activity 1-4	Message on a Bottle	page 16
Activity 2-4	To Whom It May Concern	page 51
Activity 2-5	For a Code, Take Lemon Syrup	page 53
Activity 4-5	Name, Rank, and Cereal Number	page 115

C. *Guest Speakers:* Cashier; checkout bagger; supermarket manager.

D. *Field Trips:* Supermarket.

16. TELEGRAMS

A. *Ways to Get Materials:*

1. Use the telegram forms on pages 211 and 212.

2. Send a telegram to your class. This is guaranteed to heighten student interest!

B. *Ways to Use Materials:*

1. Please see

Project 8-1   Holiday Telegrams: A First-   page 207
                Class Business

C. *Guest Speakers:* Telegraph office clerk.

D. *Field Trips:* Telegraph office.

17. TELEPHONE ITEMS

A. *Ways to Get Materials:*

1. Use the phone book yellow page on page 113 and the message forms on page 77.

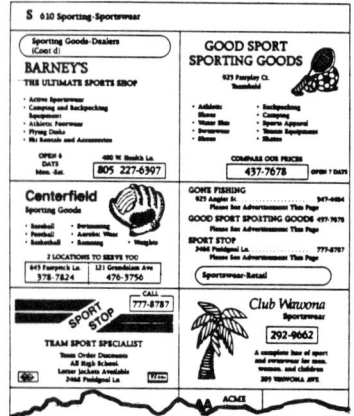 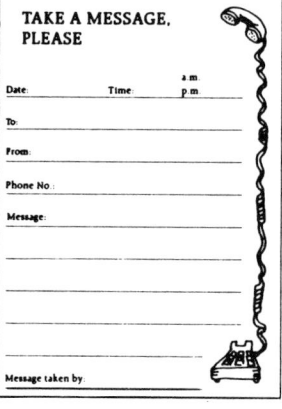

2. Ask parents to send in their old copies of the phone book when the new edition comes out. (See the sample letter on page 251.)

3. Duplicate a page from the telephone book so that everyone in the class will have a copy of the same page. (Print yellow page copies on yellow paper for a more realistic look.)

4. Call your local telephone company to find out about special equipment that amplifies the sound of a person's voice so that the whole class can hear it (see page 254).

B. *Ways to Use Materials:*

1. Please see

Activity 2-7	A Classy Phone Book	page 61
Activity 3-1	Take a Message, Please	page 75
Activity 4-4	Let Your Fingers Do the Jogging	page 111

2. Use the special telephone hook-up to interview local business people who might not otherwise be able to speak to your class. (See Activity 5-4, "Career Connection—The Interview," page 139, and Project 8-5, "Career Day," page 226.)

C. *Guest Speakers:* Telephone operator; telephone company worker.

D. *Field Trips:* Local telephone company.

18. TELEVISION SCHEDULES

A. *Ways to Get Materials:*

1. Send a letter to parents (page 251) asking them to save this week's television guide and/or the television supplement to the Sunday paper. The best time to send the letter home is Friday, asking them to send it to school on Monday.

2. In some towns, local businesses publish an advertising brochure that also contains a TV schedule. Check your local supermarket or drug and discount centers for them. Sometimes you can get enough for everyone in your class.

3. If all else fails, you can always use your own TV schedule to make copies of one or more pages.

B. *Ways to Use Materials:*

1. Please see

   Activity 6-3   The Guide Game   page 165

2. Have students use the TV schedule to classify different types of shows (comedy, documentary, news, drama, and so on).

C. *Guest Speakers:* TV or radio station announcer, programmer, or engineer.

D. *Field Trips:* Local TV or radio station.

19. TRAVEL BROCHURES

A. *Ways to Get Materials:*

1. Use the travel brochure on pages 35 and 36.

2. Ask local travel agencies to donate copies of travel brochures. (See the sample letter on page 252.)

B. *Ways to Use Materials:*

1. Please see

   Activity 1-10   Sell Your Setting   page 33

2. Use a travel brochure with an opaque projector. Ask questions about adjectives used, proper nouns, compound words, and so on.

C. *Guest Speakers:* Travel agent; hotel manager; tour guide.

D. *Field Trips:* Travel agency.

20. WARRANTIES

A. *Ways to Get Materials:*

1. Make copies of warranties from products you have purchased.
2. Ask parents to save old warranties from home appliances. Use the letter on page 251.

B. *Ways to Use Materials:*

1. Please see

   Activity 1-9   The Warranty Game   page 29
2. Make a transparency of a warranty for use on an overhead projector. Ask questions about expiration dates, parts covered, conditions, and so on.

C. *Guest Speakers:* Appliance or stereo store manager; car salesperson.

D. *Field Trips:* Appliance store; car dealership; repair shop.

List of Real-World Reading and Language Arts Games

ACTIVITY NUMBER	GAME	PAGE
1-9	The Warranty Game	29
2-8	Name That Word	63
3-8	The Energy User Game	89
4-3	The "I Care" Game	109
4-8	Supermarket B-I-M-G-O	123
5-1	Career Pursuit	133
6-3	The Guide Game	165
7-4	Cut Ups!	193

Teaching Aids

Game Spinner
(Use for Activities 1-9, 2-8, 4-3, 5-1, 6-3.)

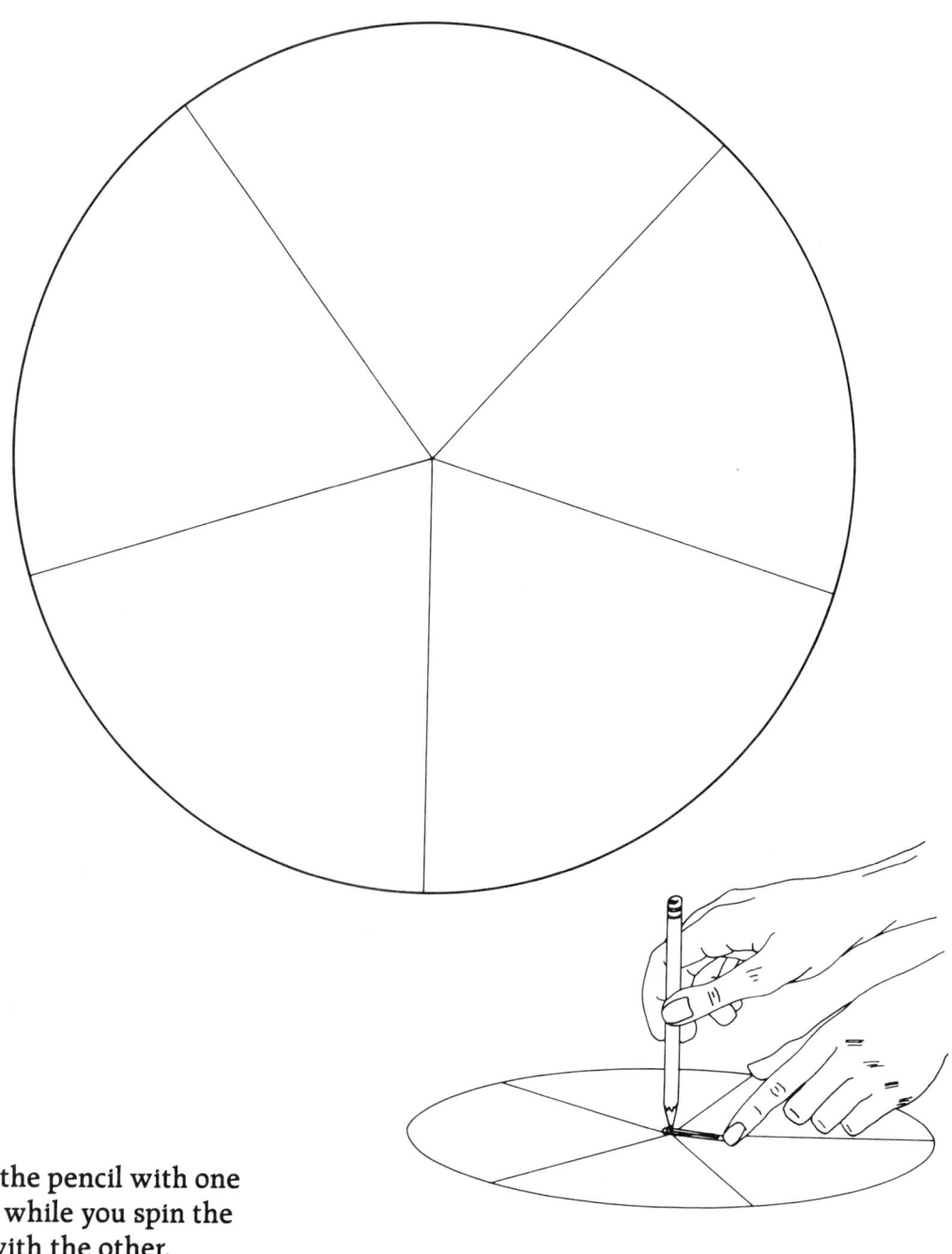

Hold the pencil with one
hand while you spin the
clip with the other.

Chapter 10: Materials and Resources

Game Board
(Use for Activities 1-9, 2-8, 4-3, 6-3.)

START

IF YOUR MOVE FINISHES HERE

MOVE ACROSS

IF YOUR MOVE FINISHES HERE

MOVE ACROSS

FINISH

Award Certificate

REAL-WORLD READING / LANGUAGE ARTS

CERTIFICATE

NAME

DATE

TEACHER

Award Certificate

READ ALL ABOUT IT!

A SMART CONSUMER

STUDENTS RECEIVE READING/
LANGUAGE ARTS AWARDS

PRESENTED TO:

_____

DATE:

_____

TEACHER:

_____

We Brought the Whole World in Our Class

(Tune: "He's Got the Whole World in His Hand")

Chorus:

> We brought the whole world in our class,
> We brought the whole(wide) world in our class,
> We brought the whole world in our class,
> We brought the whole world in our class.

We read of gates, skates and axes, and Lincoln logs,
And paper plates, dates, and waxes in catalogs.
We read the freight weights and taxes in catalogs.
We brought the whole world in our class.

[Chorus]

We demonstrated debater tips, in our class.
We evaluated computer chips, in our class.
We navigated freighter trips, in our class.
We brought the whole world in our class.

[Chorus]

We took a stance on jobs and salaries, in our class.
We took a glance at art in galleries, in our class.
We took a chance on counting calories, in our class.
We took the whole world in our class.

[Chorus]

We talked of fees on skis and cheddar cheese, in our class.
Poppies, bees, teas, and fleur-de-lis, in our class.
We've heard the pleas, "Say, please!" of agencies, in our class.
We brought the real world in our class.

We studied real-world reading and language arts,
We studied real-world reading and language arts,
We studied real-world reading and language arts,
We brought the whole world in our class.

Happiness is Real-World Reading and Language Arts!

Skills Index

Skills Index

(Numbers after entries refer to Activity numbers.)

Composing (see Writing)

Comprehension
    classifying, 1-7, 2-8, 2-10A, 4-5, 4-9A, 6-4,
        6-6, 8-3
    codes, 2-5, 2-6, 5-9D
    comparing and contrasting, 1-1, 1-2, 1-5,1-6,
        7-7J, 8-3
    details, 1-3, 1-4, 1-8, 1-9, 2-10A, 2-10H, 4-9C
    drawing conclusions, 1-2, 1-4
    following directions, 1-3, 1-8, 1-9, 2-5, 4-3,
        5-5, 5-6, 7-1
    main idea, 1-4, 1-6
    sequence of events, 3-3, 6-1

Creative Expression, 1-10, 2-1, 2-2, 2-3, 2-6, 3-6,
    3-7, 3-9H, 4-6, 4-7, 5-2, 5-3, 6-5, 6-6, 6-7,
    6-8B, 7-1, 7-2, 7-3, 7-5, 8-1, 8-2, 8-4

Critical Thinking
    analyzing information, 1-4, 4-9F, 5-9B, 5-9C
    classifying, 3-8, 4-6, 4-8, 5-1, 5-9I, 7-7C, 7-7D
    comparing and contrasting, 3-7, 3-8, 4-5, 4-6,
        4-9H, 5-1, 6-8C, 7-6
    evaluating advertisements, 3-7, 3-9B, 3-9H,
        4-4, 4-7, 4-9E,4-9H
    expressing opinions, 1-6, 3-5, 3-6, 3-7, 3-9A,
        3-9E, 3-9F, 4-7, 4-9B, 4-9H, 7-6, 8-3, 8-5
    fact and opinion, 1-11G
    factual and persuasive writing, 1-1, 2-10E

Drama, 3-7, 4-1, 5-3
    role playing, 3-1, 3-4, 3-9A, 3-9D, 3-9E, 4-4,
        5-4, 8-1, 8-4

Grammar and Usage
    adjectives, 1-11A, 2-1, 2-10B, 3-7, 3-9G, 4-1,
        4-4, 4-5, 4-7, 6-2, 6-8E, 7-3
    adverbs, 2-1, 6-2
    nouns, 2-1
    proper nouns, 4-1, 6-8E
    sentences, 2-4, 4-4, 4-5, 4-6, 5-2, 6-5, 8-5
    verbs, 1-11F, 2-1, 3-9G, 6-2, 7-4, 8-3

(Numbers after entries refer to Activity numbers.)

Handwriting, 1-10, 2-3, 2-4, 2-7, 4-1, 4-2, 4-3, 4-5,
    5-7, 6-4, 6-7, 7-1, 7-3, 7-5, 8-1, 8-2, 8-4, 8-6

Listening
    critical listening, 3-4, 3-5, 3-6, 3-7, 3-8, 5-3
    following directions, 5-8, 6-4
    listening for information, 1-3, 1-6, 1-8, 3-1,
        5-4, 8-5

Literary Skills
    setting, 1-10

Mechanics of Writing
    capitalization, 2-4, 4-5, 4-6, 6-1, 6-5, 8-5
    punctuation, 2-4, 4-5, 4-6, 6-1, 6-5, 8-5

Nonverbal Communication, 7-4
    body language, 3-2
    mime, 3-2, 3-9C

Speaking
    doing commercials, 8-2
    giving a report, 1-6, 8-6
    giving directions, 2-9
    giving information, 1-3, 3-1, 8-1
    interviewing, 5-4, 8-2, 8-5, 8-6
    making introductions, 3-9I, 8-5
    ordering from a menu, 4-1
    sharing experiences, 8-4
    using the telephone, 3-9D, 4-4, 5-3, 5-4

Spelling, 1-5, 1-10, 2-2, 2-3, 2-4, 2-6, 2-9, 2-10F,
    3-1, 4-1, 4-2, 4-3, 4-5, 4-8, 5-1, 5-2, 5-3, 5-5,
    5-6, 6-5, 6-7, 6-8D, 7-1, 7-3, 7-5, 8-4, 8-5, 8-6

Study Skills
    alphabetical order, 1-11B, 2-7, 4-4, 4-5
    bar graphs, 6-5, 8-6
    catalogs, 1-3, 4-2, 4-9D
    charts, 4-9G
    classified ads, 1-7, 8-3
    diagrams, 5-2
    dictionary, 4-1
    flow charts, 3-3
    index, 1-3, 4-2
    invoices, 6-4

S K I L L S I N D E X

(Numbers after entries refer to Activity numbers.)

job applications, 5-5
line graphs, 8-6
maps, 2-9, 6-7, 8-6
newspapers, 1-5, 1-7, 2-2, 8-3
order forms, 4-2
schedules, 5-8, 6-3, 6-8F, 8-1
skimming, 1-5, 6-2, 8-3
taking notes, 2-9
telephone books, 2-7, 4-4
surveys, 8-6

Vocabulary
abbreviations, 1-5, 2-2, 2-10H, 4-4, 4-5, 8-3
antonyms, 4-7
compound words, 4-1, 4-4, 5-1, 6-8E
content area words, 1-1, 1-5, 2-8, 4-8, 5-1,
        8-3, 8-5
synonyms, 6-2, 8-3
words from other languages, 4-1, 4-9F

Word Recognition
blends, 1-11D
suffixes, 1-11A
syllables, 1-11E, 4-1
vowel sounds, 1-11C

Writing
advertisements, 1-5, 2-1, 2-2, 5-3, 8-1, 8-2,
        8-3, 8-4
autobiographical sketches, 2-10E
business fliers, 5-3, 8-1
business letters, 2-4, 4-4, 4-5
catalog copy, 2-3, 4-9D
cereal box labels, 1-1
codes, 2-5, 2-6, 4-4, 5-9D
commercials, 4-5, 8-2
critiques, 6-7
descriptive paragraphs, 2-8, 5-4, 6-5, 7-5
descriptive phrases, 2-10C, 2-10H, 3-5, 3-7
dialogue, 2-3, 6-1
directions, 2-9, 3-3, 6-7

(Numbers after entries refer to Activity numbers.)

Writing *(cont.)*
    essays, 4-6, 6-7, 6-8G
    explanatory paragraphs, 5-2
    friendly letters, 2-10I
    greeting cards, 2-10I, 7-1, 7-5
    invitations, 5-4, 7-1, 8-5
    job descriptions, 5-7
    letters
        business, 2-4, 4-4, 4-5
        friendly, 2-10E, 2-10I
    lost and found notices, 2-10H
    menus, 4-1
    messages, 3-1, 4-4
    news reports, 8-2, 8-5
    paragraphs
    descriptive, 5-4, 6-5, 7-5
    explanatory, 5-2
    phrases, 7-2, 7-7E
        descriptive, 2-10C, 3-5, 3-7, 7-7F, 7-7G
    poems, 2-10B, 7-3, 7-7B, 7-7H
    post cards, 1-10
    product labels, 8-2
    programs, 8-5
    reports, 8-6
    résumés, 5-6
    sentences, 2-10D, 5-9A, 7-7A
    song lyrics, 3-6
    summaries, 1-6, 8-3, 8-5
    telegrams, 2-10I, 8-1
    thank-you notes, 5-4, 7-7H
    travel brochures, 1-10